D1571090

Advance Praise for
Money in the Streets

"Barry has taught and inspired many people as a speaker, and now, in his new book, he's able to reach and positively influence the lives of many more. *Money in the Streets* teaches you how to find and identify the opportunities everyone else is missing, as well as use them to strengthen your personal and business relationships to attain the success you deserve."

—TONY ROBBINS,
#1 *New York Times* Bestselling Author,
Philanthropist, and Peak Performance Strategist

MONEY IN THE
STREETS

MONEY IN THE STREETS

A Playbook for Finding and Seizing the Opportunity All Around You

BARRY HABIB

SAVIO
REPVBLIC

A SAVIO REPUBLIC BOOK
An Imprint of Post Hill Press

Money in the Streets:
A Playbook for Finding and Seizing the Opportunity All Around You
© 2020 by Barry Habib
All Rights Reserved

ISBN: 978-1-64293-632-2
ISBN (eBook): 978-1-64293-633-9

Cover design by Sooraj Mathew
Edited by Hilary Jastram, Dan Habib, Donna Zuckerberg & Jen Rothke
Contributions by Bookmark Editing House
Interior design and composition, Greg Johnson, Textbook Perfect

posthillpress.com
New York • Nashville
Published in the United States of America

DEDICATION

*For Mom and Dad and all the sacrifices you made
to give me opportunity.*

For Tina and Norm, for all your support.

*For Dan, Nicole, Jake, and Jared, for being the inspiration
and driving force for me to want to succeed.*

CONTENTS

Part Three: How to Use Your Opportunities in the Service of Others

FOREWORD

There are two types of people in this world. There are the people who change others' lives, then take entirely too much credit for it, and there are the people who change others' lives and allow the benefit of that positive change to be its own reward. Barry embodies the latter. He doesn't need to boast about his accomplishments because his impression on people lasts way longer than any accolade ever would.

Barry came into my life when he and the producers of *Rock of Ages* offered me a role in their show. I'd dreamed of being involved with Broadway my entire life, but it wasn't happening for me in any traditional sense. Finally, in 2014, I was offered the role of Regina, and Barry changed my entire career trajectory. Without ever knowing it, Barry helped better not only my life but the lives of so many other aspiring Broadway babies because now I'm an active investor in other people's dreams—as he was once in mine.

Barry is inspiring to people both professionally and personally. He believes if he can overcome his own unfortunate circumstances, anyone can. He's a true entrepreneur—he practices what he preaches. He doesn't shy away from the challenges he has faced or the incredible hardships he has endured. Instead, he uses his stories to inspire other people. He possesses an intense loyalty to family—and by "family," I don't just mean blood relatives. I mean all of those who live under the protective umbrella of our lives.

From the moment I first met Barry to the present day, I've witnessed his inspiring, unconditional love for his umbrella family. He'll spot someone in need and immediately take them under his wing. That's why I love *Money in the Streets*. It's 100 percent, Barry, in all his infinite love, providing a step-by-step road map to alter the circumstances of life. Learning how to stay grounded, express gratitude, and live in service of others will make you more successful. And I know this is true because it's a lesson that Barry taught me five years ago. It lives within me every day and is the backbone of how I lead, learn, and love.

Barry can help you to be a better you too. Just turn the page.

#withlove
Randi Zuckerberg

INTRODUCTION

As a professional speaker, I've always tried to be selective about the speaking engagements that I commit to. But it wasn't always that way.

Early on in my career, I was anxious to have speaking opportunities. One time, in particular, I agreed to do a speaking engagement as a favor for someone. This meant that I would not collect a speaking fee and would only be reimbursed for my expenses. After agreeing to do the gig, I started researching flights. Because this engagement was in Santa Fe, New Mexico, and I was in New Jersey, it was a total pain in the ass to get to.

If you've ever had to take connecting flights, you know what a hassle it is. Well, this trip had two connecting flights, a rental car, a long drive, and a ferry ride. Just kidding about the ferry ride. But there might as well have been one.

The day before I was supposed to travel, I was not feeling well. But I had made a commitment, so I forced myself, reluctantly, to make the trek to Santa Fe for free while feeling miserable. Little did I know that this opportunity would change the course of my life.

The venue was not the greatest. I knew I was in trouble when I checked in and found that the cost of the room was only $25 per night! To top it off, the hotel provided a coupon for a free beer for each night's stay. I remember asking the hotel clerk if he could please charge me a little more so I could feel more confident about the accommodations.

The next morning, I was surprised to see that there was a solid turnout for the event, and I proceeded to give my keynote talk.

At the event, there were three different people who were especially interested in what I had to say. Each came up individually to speak with me after my talk. One has turned out to be a dear friend to this day. Another was the head of the largest mortgage insurance company in the U.S. (which wound up sponsoring me for a national four-year-long speaking tour). The third became my business partner in a venture that we later sold for millions of dollars.

Opportunities are truly everywhere, and I might have lost out on some of these life-changing opportunities if I hadn't been able to identify them. I simply wouldn't even know all the great things I was missing. Identifying opportunities is a skill that can be learned and sharpened. It's an important skill to harness because it's scary to think about all of the opportunities that we have missed out on in our lives, not because we didn't take advantage of them, but because we never saw them in the first place.

In this book, I want to share with you how to first identify your opportunities, then how you can take advantage of them to improve your life and the lives of those around you. The opportunities I'm talking about can be related to business or your personal finances, but they can also be about the relationships that make our lives special. Some opportunities can also help us grow personally.

I've learned so many life lessons through my relationships and experiences. But these lessons don't just apply to me. I'm pretty sure they'll apply to you too.

My experiences in each chapter of this book have been specifically translated into lessons that you can use to enrich and enhance *your* life.

You will make a deep connection to many sections within the book. And if you take the lessons I share and apply them in your interactions with others, as well as to build your business, you will achieve significantly greater success—and even more importantly, you will attain that success with fulfillment. *Remember, you need both to be happy.*

Life is about relationships. And relationships are about people. Our interactions with others make us who we are and tell us how we feel about ourselves. Understanding ourselves better helps us reach higher levels of success and fulfillment.

Money in the Streets is a phrase that means there are opportunities all around us that others are passing by. They just don't know the trick yet, which is how to first look for opportunities and then make the most of them.

After reading this book, you'll know how to do both and want to teach others how to do the same. I think you'll want to read this book more than once to use as a guide to help you through difficult times and as a playbook to maximize the good times yet to come.

Success and fulfillment aren't exclusive to those who've started off with everything in their lives handed to them on a silver platter.... I sure wasn't one of those lucky ones. As you'll come to see, I grew up extremely poor and can relate to what it's like to have both financial and family struggles. Overcoming those early disadvantages has given me the perspective and experience that I will share with you. These lessons will help you lift yourself from wherever you may be or from whatever you are currently facing to take you to a better place. While these are my stories and lessons, they aren't *about* me as much as they come *through* me.

If I can overcome the disadvantages that I've faced, I'm quite certain that you'll be able to overcome your challenges as well—even if it doesn't seem that way right now.

This book will help you identify and cultivate habits that will bring you success. But there are also common characteristics that many people possess that create more challenges in life than necessary—and there are feelings that hold them back from the life they deserve. In the pages that follow, you will learn how to foster more success while understanding and defeating self-limiting beliefs.

If you have ever been held back by fear, indecision, or confusion, *Money in the Streets* will help you. Once you get past those obstacles, you'll set your sights on attaining levels of success and fulfillment beyond what you thought possible, and *Money in the Streets* will help you reach those heights too.

If you want more in your life,

if you want greater success

no matter where you are,

but mostly,

if you want to do good for others with your success, then you're the person I want reading this book, because...

You have the power to change the world.

PART ONE

How to See Opportunity Everywhere

CHAPTER 1

Overcoming the Random Nature of Rejection

"The more rejection you get, the better you are, the more you've learned, the closer you are to your outcome.... If you can handle rejection, you'll learn to get everything you want."

—TONY ROBBINS

Random.

It's a word that we use quite often, but do we realize that it describes how each of us entered this world?

We don't get to pick our entry point. We don't get to pick the country, the language, or the climate. We enter, as if through a time machine, into a period of time that we have no control over. We could have just as easily been born five hundred years ago or maybe five hundred years into the future. We had no choice in the matter.

The way we enter this world is the most random event we will ever experience. Nothing throughout the rest of our lives will compare. And because there is no choice in this matter, our lives are all about what we do with what we get. We enter this world with a slap on the ass and take it from there.

Maybe we're born into wealthy families, or maybe we're born into families that are struggling and poor like my family was. I didn't choose to come into a struggling set of circumstances, but in order to not just "make the most of things" but to succeed and persevere, I had to understand that even though I had experienced difficulties, I didn't have to accept that my circumstances would always remain this way.

Like you, my random entry was unique. In fact, I almost didn't enter at all. I really was not supposed to be here. I wasn't just unplanned; I was unwanted.

My parents had just arrived in the U.S. and were broke. They already had two teenaged kids to look after, and finding work was hard. Adding to the stress was the fact that they didn't speak English, didn't have anyone to help, and were older. And by older, I mean *older*, especially compared to the age of people having kids back then. When I was born, Dad was fifty-seven, and Mom was approaching forty. After learning that Mom was pregnant, my parents didn't think they could handle starting over with another child, especially with all the other aforementioned challenges.

But just as my conception was random, so was the timing and unlikely inspiration that would end up bringing me into this world. I'll get to that in a bit.

I don't blame my parents for not planning or wanting another child, given their circumstances. I'd probably feel the same way. But I still had to overcome the feeling of rejection, which is something I had to learn about early on. Even though I made it into this world, my parents' challenges became my challenges too.

When I was a young boy, I had to translate for my mother. She was a very intelligent woman, however, even though she did not speak English at the time. Mom spoke *six* languages, including Spanish, French, Italian, Turkish, and Greek. This is a very impressive accomplishment under any circumstance, but it's truly amazing when you consider that she never learned to read or write. You see, when she was a young girl, she was pulled out of school because her mother became very ill and she had to fulfill family duties.

But as I was saying, as a child, I had to translate for her with our landlord and shopkeepers as well as my teachers—although I may have left out some of the bad stuff my teachers used to say. I really was a handful in school. I was a good kid and a bright one, but I was also a jokester and prankster and often found myself in the principal's office.

Sometimes, for example, I'd get a few friends to launch a coordinated effort of making paper airplanes so we could fire them all at once when the teacher turned his back to write on the blackboard. And one time, I wound up in the principal's office for causing a stir in science class. Do you know what happens when you drop dry sulfuric acid in water? It causes a small explosion...and it also causes you to get sent to the principal's office.

I think I liked playing pranks and joking around because it made me feel like I fit in better with my classmates.

Nevertheless, almost every day, when I came home from school, I remember going through the mail and being a little overwhelmed at needing to figure out what all the adult writing meant—after all, I was just an eleven-year-old kid. Yes, there were more responsibilities I had to take on, but after every interaction where I'd have to handle some sort of business for my family, my confidence grew.

Also, because we were very poor, I didn't have toys except for the ones that other kids discarded, so I *had* to be creative. I played with matchbooks (I used to flick them across the table to make field goals), rolled socks into balls and threw them into a lampshade when I played house basketball (Mom wasn't too crazy about that one), and used my imagination.

Every experience of making something from nothing fostered my creativity.

While I sure wasn't part of the silver-spoon club, I was still happy. I always believed in something better—something bigger. I dreamed all the time. And I let myself fall deep inside those dreams, so they felt like a reality. It wasn't a question of whether I'd get there—it was a matter of when I would.

I knew we wouldn't always struggle or be invisible. I felt in my heart that good things were ahead. I was optimistic and had a positive outlook. And from a very early age, my mom taught me to be kind to others. Even though we had next to nothing, my mom would always manage to find a way to help someone less fortunate.

As we'd ride the subway in New York City, I came to recognize the look in her eyes that said she was about to take out her gold-colored change purse and offer a few coins to help someone in need. Each time she did this, she would make sure to tell me, "It's good to help people."

Kindness is contagious.

It will uplift the people to whom kindness is shown and inspire them to be kind in return, causing an amazing ripple effect. But being kind to others will also uplift the spirit of the person who is sending out the kind gestures. It's the perfect example of getting more by giving. It gave me more energy and optimism.

Even though we were very poor, we could still be helpful and kind. We didn't have to be bitter and resentful. We didn't have to be jealous of those who had more. Just because we were poor didn't mean we had to be unhappy.

My first real lesson was that:

"MINDSET IS EVERYTHING."

My ancestors were from Spain, but several generations had settled in Turkey, which was not an easy place for my family to be. They had heard incredible things about America, including that "America is such a rich country, there's *money in the streets*. All you have to do is reach down and pick it up." So many immigrants have heard this very same tale about America's riches.

Later, my parents chuckled when they repeated that saying to me, talking about how ridiculous it was to believe that there was *real* money in the streets. And sometimes, it wasn't ridiculous; it was sad.

I remember vividly one day when my mom was walking up the stairs to where we lived, which was a couple of flights up. When she reached our door, the grocery bag she was holding suddenly broke. She started crying and said, "Before coming here, I heard all these stories about how America was so rich that there was money in the streets...." I felt so helpless, seeing her cry and witnessing her exhaustion after a tough day of working in the sweatshop. I crouched down to collect the groceries that were now at her feet. As I helped her gather up the spilled food, I wished I could do something that would eventually make it easier for her.

My parents arrived in Brooklyn, New York, in 1958, with my older brother Norman and my sister Tina, six suitcases, and not an English word in their vocabulary. The Turkish government had taken almost everything they had as the price for leaving. Ninety-four percent of their financial worth was confiscated, leaving them with almost nothing to start a new life in America.

I have two older brothers from my dad's first marriage, David and Rafi. They did not come to the U.S. when my parents did and instead decided to check out this new country, Israel. Since they were both in their twenties, it made sense for them to start their own lives.

David later came to the U.S. with his family, which included his son, Avi. Years later, Avi started working with me, and he continues to do so to this very day.

When my parents originally arrived here, though, they were mostly on their own. With so many disadvantages, navigating the new country was a challenge—one that was far more difficult back then than it would be today. They were disparaged, talked down to, and discriminated against in the workforce. The social rules that are in effect today to prevent marginalization and inform the way you talk to or treat someone did not protect them back then. When I witnessed this treatment, it broke my heart.

Although my parents found work, the work left much to be desired. In Turkey, my dad had been an international journalist. But in America, because he didn't yet speak English, Dad found work to support his family at a hot dog stand. My mom worked at a sweatshop making dresses. Norman picked up work wherever he could to help, but whatever he earned went to the household to contribute to paying bills. This was very different than what most teenagers were accustomed to doing with their money.

I can't imagine how difficult it must've been for my family to swallow their pride and make the sacrifices necessary to survive. They didn't exactly find the abundance in America that everyone was talking about.

Things got really interesting in 1959 when my mom became pregnant with me. As I mentioned, she was nearly forty years old, and my dad was fifty-seven; they were barely making ends meet. Now they had discovered that there was a baby on the way.

They considered abortion, and I can understand why. It must have been so scary facing those unknowns. Fortunately for me, abortion was illegal back then. Even more fortunately for me, I was conceived in 1959. That's important to note because birth control pills came on the scene just a few months later in 1960. Talk about just making it!

Mom didn't know what to do. I don't begrudge my mom and dad for thinking about such a drastic alternative. Instead, I am just thrilled with being here! That might be part of the reason why I feel like I need to do more with my life. I almost wasn't! I'm on bonus time, and life is truly a gift!

I also understand that uncertainty can be crushing. But my mother would gain the confidence, reassurance, and inspiration to move forward after she received a very unusual proposition.

One day, early in her pregnancy, my mom was at work on her machine. She was just one dressmaker sitting in a line—just one line among lines and lines of people working in cramped and suffocating conditions. The stress of her situation got to her, and she cried while she sewed.

"Why are you so upset? Why are you crying?" her boss, Emma, asked as she walked up to her. Emma owned the shop with her husband, Joe.

Mom glanced up at Emma, tears trickling down her cheeks. "I don't know what I'm going to do," she cried as more tears spilled from her eyes. "We have a baby coming, and we have no money. We're not young. How will we do it?" Mom wiped her eyes on her sleeve and tried to stop her sobs. She was at work, after all, and it wasn't the most comfortable place to have such a conversation.

"Listen," Emma said. "I've tried all my life to have a baby, and I can't. If you want, if you have the baby, you can give it to me. I'll take it, and I'll go away." Emma's words came out so fast, and Mom's stomach clenched at the thought of losing the baby inside her forever. She knew in that moment what to do as Emma continued, and Mom grew more horrified over this odd proposition. "You'll never have to worry," Emma continued, now leaning in close, her hands on her knees and the light of possibility in her eyes. Mom could see on her boss's face that she meant every word she said. Emma was already imagining her future as a mother. Whether Mom kept her beautiful baby that she didn't yet know how she would take care of came down to one word... either yes or no. Emma was so close to having what she'd always wanted, and my mom was the person who could give it to her. Mom forced herself to finish listening to what she now knew was a crazy scheme: "I'll give you money. You can even have the business," Emma pleaded.

Emma was willing to trade everything for what my mother already had. At that moment, my mom came to see the pregnancy as a blessing. It gave her the inspiration to be happy about it. She realized how lucky she was and what other people would give to have the opportunity that she'd been given. Amazingly, just changing her perspective and her mindset changed her entire world.

She politely told her boss, "No, thank you," and went back to work, losing herself and her shaky state of mind in the white noise of the machines roaring and punching through fabric.

I came into this world loved and wanted because my mother was able to change her mindset, to see what she had as a blessing. This is an important life lesson for all of us. When you change your perspective, you change your life.

Years later, Emma came to visit my mom and me at our house. When she saw me as a young man, she turned to my mom and said, "You made the right decision."

When I learned of this story, I refused to focus on the fact that I had been up for grabs before I had even been born. Instead, I turned my focus to how stressful an unexpected pregnancy must've felt to my parents. I didn't make it about me, and that's the trick. Rejection doesn't *have* to be about you. It's often due to the circumstances that others are going through and the pressures they are feeling.

Rejection can just be a result of a random situation. But the way you deal with it depends on your mindset, which remains totally within your control.

CHAPTER 2

Let Hardship Teach You

"At the end of hardship, comes happiness."

—KOREAN PROVERB

Tony Robbins has been a huge inspiration for me. He's also a brilliant professional speaker. As a speaker myself, I've been blessed with the ability to be a very good communicator, but I always work to improve and make changes to stay relevant. And I've learned so much from Tony—not just from his message, but also from his delivery, the connection he makes with his audience, and the empathy that he has for others. His sincere desire to help people make a positive difference in their lives is on par with some of the most groundbreaking mindset work this century. Tony is at the pinnacle of the speaking profession, and I truly cherish that I can call him a friend.

I remember Tony walking over to me through a sea of 3,000 people who were hanging on his every word at one of his events. Laying his hand on my shoulder, he addressed the audience, his voice booming in the auditorium: "Barry Habib's a very successful guy. But he will have hardships and suffer too." The best way to move through the challenges we will all face is to have what Tony calls "a beautiful mindset." You will suffer much less if your view of the world comes from gratitude.

Having the strength to overcome hardships doesn't mean that you ride off into the sunset without a care in the world. There will always be more challenges ahead, regardless of who you are. Sometimes, when we interact with successful people, all we see are their wins. But nobody's life is perfect all of the time, no matter what their social media feed might tell you.

The truth is we all have hardships.

What defines us is how we respond to those hardships. You can let them ruin you, or you can let them teach you. You can let them stop you, or you can move through those challenging times and come out better for it on the other side.

If you can face adversity and learn from it, then you have a true superpower. Since there's no shortage of adversity, that means you have a never-ending source of strength.

When I was growing up, I didn't have to look very far to find hardships. I knew what poverty looked like. Poverty looked like the five of us sharing a two-bedroom apartment with one bathroom. (Since my brother and sister were teenagers, you can guess who had to wait for the bathroom.)

Poverty looked like kids making fun of my hand-me-down clothes that didn't fit right and didn't look right. It looked like being on the outer rim of belonging to a community. It looked like being different and never being able to forget it. That feeling stays with me every day and fuels my desire to help others so they won't have to feel the same way.

You can guess how my mindset lifted me out of those realities during that time.

I also struggled with people's perceptions of my dad, who was much older than most other fathers. I remember being asked, "Is that your grandfather?" It was so embarrassing that I wished I could disappear. And it wasn't just the comments about the age difference that mortified me. It was also the way my parents mispronounced words or misinterpreted things. I couldn't help but hear the snickering of the other kids.

In a world where English was *the* language, I was on my own, including when I was doing my homework because no one could help me.

Many of my friends came home to a mom waiting with cookies and help for their homework assignments. I arrived home to an empty house. I could always visit my mom at the sweatshop, though, and I did when I missed her the most...or, like most kids, when I wanted something.

I remember the roar of the machines. I remember how hard the women worked, how hard it was to meet the demands of the work. I remember them hunched over their stitching, their sharp eyes assessing any stitch out of place, and I remember that sense of solidarity. All the ladies, many of whom were likely mothers themselves, smiled when I walked into the stifling room.

When some of them would see my little bobbing head appear over their piles of fabric as I walked by looking for my mom, they would yell to her, "Korina, Korina!" Her head would snap around in my direction with a big smile. Everyone was always happy to see me. It gave them a distraction from the machines they were figuratively shackled to.

Since Mom worked so much, my sister Tina took care of me. She tried to fill in for my mom as best as she could so the house wouldn't always feel so empty. Our little family found a system, and we got by until we were hit by another hardship that changed me forever.

When I was eleven years old, my dad had a heart attack. I didn't really understand what a heart attack was, and I certainly didn't know how serious it could be. He survived but ended up in the hospital.

My family visited him as soon as he was stable. I don't remember much about what was talked about during that visit, but I do remember that he looked okay to me. *Maybe a heart attack wasn't that bad? After all, he had survived!*

We wrapped up our goodbyes and headed toward the elevator. But when I got there, I froze. A feeling of needing to go back to my dad's room came over me. My feet refused to budge as my family waited for the elevator. Suddenly, I bolted back down the hallway to Dad's room to say goodbye again. I ran to his room as quickly as I could because I knew my family was waiting for me. Dad and I made short but intense eye contact as he lay there, and I was slightly breathless as I said, "Bye, Daddy."

I will treasure that brief goodbye forever. That was the last time I ever saw him.

I am so grateful for whatever feeling forced me back to his side. I trusted my gut—something I would learn to do more and more throughout my life.

Dad was fine throughout the night, but the next day, he had another heart attack. This time, he didn't make it.

Nothing would ever be the same again.

Without my father, I had to grow up really fast. I was the baby in the family, and by this time, my siblings were married and living in New Jersey—not exactly around the corner from our apartment in Brooklyn. It was just my mom and me on our own.

I was eleven, and she was illiterate.

Her job at the sweatshop paid our bills, but without my dad, I had to help her with many basic activities. When we'd make the long drive to visit my siblings, I would have to navigate. Anything that required reading fell to me.

So, yes, we struggled, but through it all, I was happy. I get my fighting spirit and positive outlook from my mom, and we refused to let the loss of my father destroy our lives.

And although I don't think anyone would *choose* to be poor, we made the most of it.

Sometimes, when I talk about my childhood, people ask: "Would you change anything to make it easier?"

I know my answer without even thinking about it. *Never*.

I don't lose myself in "poor me" even when, to the outside world, that might seem logical. I don't want to be in that mindset. It doesn't give me anything, and it takes me away from what I am supposed to be doing on this planet—helping and inspiring others.

It also gave me the empathy to understand other people's struggles—a trait that I've been mindful of passing onto my own children.

As a parent, I may have occasionally been guilty of spoiling my children. I wanted them to have what I was never able to have. And I found their joy—the smiles on their faces and their pure, innocent happiness—simply intoxicating! I assumed, as a person coming from a background of not having much, that my kids' gratitude would be baked-in like mine.

But one day, my son Dan made a negative remark about a friend of his who didn't have as much as we did. I stopped him and said, "Dan, that boy you're making fun of was once me. And if you're going to make fun of him, it's just like you're making fun of me."

I saw his perspective shift in that moment. Dan gasped as he stared up at me with guilt and sadness in his eyes. "Sorry, Daddy."

I told him, "It's okay, buddy. I just wanted you to know so you can be kind to other kids who might not be as fortunate as you." Then I held my arms open as I crouched to embrace him. He walked into my hug, and all was right with the world.

Dan never made that remark again, and neither did my daughter Nicole, who had overheard the conversation. When she learned her daddy had struggled, her sweet face registered the same shock as Dan's.

It wasn't my intention to make Dan feel bad about it. He had learned the lesson, and it has stayed with both him and Nicole to this day. They know they shouldn't think they're better than those who have less, and they understand that, due to random circumstances, they just might be luckier.

And, therefore, maybe those who have less should be more deserving of our compassion and kindness.

I would not be here today without the lessons my early life taught me, and I have come to appreciate those challenges as they have helped shape me. I even appreciate those times where I passed the lessons onto my kids, although it hurt a little to do so.

We can all use adversity to find solutions and develop resilience. What started out as disadvantages taught me how to gain and harness skills that have helped me throughout my life. If I had been given everything, I might not have had to learn anything.

When we get sick, our body produces antibodies that make us more resistant to getting sick the next time and help us stay healthy in the future. It's helpful for me to view life in this way. Maybe it's helpful for you to do the same.

You don't need to welcome pain, but you can always cherish the lessons and opportunities to improve your life. The trick is recognizing them.

CHAPTER 3

Find Opportunity

"Finding opportunity is a matter
of believing it's there."

—BARBARA CORCORAN

Even when life is challenging, it's important to remember that opportunity is everywhere. My earliest opportunities came from the lessons that my hardships taught me. Then I took what I learned and started to build a life.

Looking at my career now, you probably wouldn't guess that my first job, while in high school, was working in a butcher store. That was the first time I learned that you could work hard and have fun too. The owner exemplified this idea when he handed me my shirt (uniform) to wear, which proudly said: "You can beat our prices, but you can't beat our meat!"

From there, I sold calculators in college. Every student needed a fancy calculator, and they didn't come cheap. I saw a market and arranged to buy calculators in bulk and sell them at a discount to my fellow students. My idea paid for my own calculator and then some.

Once I saw how I could use sales to get ahead in life, there was no stopping me. Sales was the avenue I had been waiting for. It was the opportunity for me to find *money in the streets*.

After calculators, I sold housewares out of my trunk. I did well and put money in my pockets. One afternoon, I was at a restaurant enjoying the rewards of my success when, unbeknownst to me, my next opportunity walked through the door. He was a salesman, and I watched him as he tried to sell stereos out of the trunk of his car to the proprietor. He was older than me and more experienced, but I saw myself in him because there he was...selling in the streets, just like me.

Since I knew how hard it could be to get customers (particularly when your storefront is your car), I stepped up to help. I asked him questions that gave him a chance to talk about his product. I went on to say that it looked like he was offering a good deal.

I helped him, and he noticed.

After he made his sale, we got to talking, and I told him that I was selling housewares out of the trunk of my car. He told me selling stereos would be more lucrative. And I took him up on that advice.

This was my first experience with the law of reciprocity. Because I showed this salesman kindness and helped him, he felt obligated to reciprocate. His advice paid off quickly and took me to another level in my business.

Soon enough, I graduated from housewares to stereos. This was a solid move because speakers and radios generate a lot more income than pots and pans.

My two best childhood friends, Craig Frankel and David Augenblick, joined me in the stereo business. These two were about as crazy as they come—wonderful friends, just a bit insane. Every day was an adventure, but a fun one. They both later joined me in the mortgage business.

Selling stereos out of my trunk in different neighborhoods to strangers taught me many lessons. Most of all, I learned about persistence and resiliency—how to not let rejection stop you from pursuing your goals. I learned so much about people from talking to them and better understanding our differences. But most importantly, I learned that when bad things happen, it can be an amazing opportunity.

Electronic equipment can break or be defective right out of the box from time to time. Since cell phones didn't exist yet, I gave out a phone number to an answering service so that customers could reach me. When the inevitable problems occurred, customers would dial the service. I'm sure they thought that they would never hear from me again. But they were pleasantly surprised when I promptly responded. Then, when I drove out to either fix or exchange the product, they were shocked. It was the right thing to do. Often, the customer was so happy that they felt obligated to reciprocate by buying more products or telling others to buy from me. If everything had worked fine, they would never have learned about my character or that they could trust me. And trust is critical in building relationships. Obstacles allow you to shine, come through, and show who you really are. When things go wrong, it is often a chance to take that small setback and turn it into giant future growth. Eventually, I was making enough money to generate some savings.

Even in my twenties, I was observant, and through my travels selling stereo equipment, I noticed that property values in New Jersey offered a better opportunity than those in New York. I combined resources with a few friends and family members and began buying real estate. Some properties were new construction contract flips, which allow me to sell the contract to purchase before closing; some were purchased, renovated, and then flipped; others were held onto and rented. I learned a lot of lessons, including the power of leverage, thanks to the use of mortgages.

But those early mortgages did more than teach me that leverage can create wealth; they turned out to be one of my most significant inspirations.

The real estate bug bit me hard. I became fascinated with all things real estate, right in time to finance the birth of a new chapter in my life...literally.

In 1986, I was blessed with the birth of my twins, Nicole and Dan. When I brought the twins home, as any father would, I thought about the road ahead and my responsibility to these two new little creatures. My goal was simple: to provide for my family and eventually retire with money in the bank. As I was dabbling in real estate at the time, I saw the possibility of our family living an entirely new life.

In that moment, I was done selling stereos. I decided to start selling mortgages. That meant that I would work for a bank or mortgage company that provided loans to people who were purchasing homes and needed financing, or individuals looking to refinance their current mortgage in order to save money with a lower interest rate or to consolidate debt.

I would have to find referral sources or reach potential customers directly to assist them with their mortgage needs.

But it wasn't easy. No one wanted to trust some wet-behind-the-ears rookie kid with their mortgage. And real estate agents would be hesitant to refer me due to my youth and lack of experience.

I'll never forget my first mortgage opportunity, which came in the form of a wonderful man by the name of Milt Knochbar. I had just flipped a contract on a property that he had purchased from me. Milt was a sweet older man with hair out of place, glasses too big for his face, and warm eyes. He was slow to respond as if he were processing what he had just heard, but when he did, he did so gently and kindly. He took a liking to me. After all, I was a good kid who worked hard and treated him fairly. I told Milt I had just gotten into the mortgage business, and although I wasn't really familiar with it, I asked Milt if he would be patient and do me the honor of being my first mortgage client. He enthusiastically agreed. I sold Milt his home... and then I did his mortgage...and...yes, it's true...I also sold him a stereo for his brand-new home.

Milt was my foot in the door, but I still had to figure out how to sell more mortgages.

Mortgage professionals typically gain business by visiting real estate agents and having them refer their clients who are purchasing homes. But I was new on the scene, and realtors already had relationships. They weren't willing to give me a chance.

I had no choice but to convince these realtors that I would work hard for them and their clients—and I did. Once, I even showed a realtor a picture of little two-month-old Dan and Nicole and said, "I have no choice but to do a good job for you. I can't let down these babies." When Dan and Nicole were born, they were premature and extra tiny and fragile. You could see their miniature little limbs and peeping eyes in the picture. Poor Nicole, who has such beautiful hair today, didn't have any for quite a while. That realtor was one of the first ones who trusted me with their business.

Another realtor, Anita Sanzio, eventually started sending me referrals because she was happy with a stereo that I had previously sold her. I still talk to her.

Even with those two realtors on my side, it was very hard to gain business traction. So I decided to go out at night and knock on people's doors to sell mortgages or to convince people to refinance their existing mortgage. Rejection was a reality, and some people slammed the door in my face; others actually called the cops. But I was resilient because giving up was not an option. So in that one week, sixteen families wrote mortgages with me. This was an unheard-of number. I broke every record with those wins. I'd written more in seven days than half of the people at the company had written in a year.

But now that I had written a massive pile of loans, they had to get closed. I needed help.

Enter Holly Roth, another mentor, and much-needed support. Holly recognized my talent and helped me close those deals. She taught me the mortgage business and was quite patient. Understand, I can be an overwhelming student, and I pestered her with questions constantly. But she handled it all with grace, and I'm eternally grateful for her.

Remembering that time makes me smile. I was a young man, full of hunger and energy—or, as some people say, piss and vinegar—and I believed anything was attainable. As business picked up, I discovered that I had literally made money in the streets. I was walking those streets, pounding the pavement and putting myself out there, and the streets were paying me back. All of those years earlier, when my parents had told me how silly they'd been to believe they'd find money in the streets of America, they actually hadn't been that far off. I had finally turned that legend into a reality. Making money in the streets was about seeing the opportunities you could leverage to build wealth.

When I realized this truth, I sat down with my mom and told her, "Mom, there *is* money in the streets here."

She laughed a little at how silly it sounded. I chuckled too. But I had to make her understand that she and Dad hadn't been wrong; they just hadn't known the trick.

"It's true. It's there," I said. "But it's not just lying around on the ground, and it won't show up in your pocket. You have to know how to pick it up. You have to know how to create enough value, so people are willing to give it to you."

As I explained to her what I meant, understanding dawned in her eyes. She reached out, grabbed my hand, and gave it a squeeze. I knew she heard me. She patted my hand and nodded her head, her eyes shining and a slight smile on her elegant face. My heart swelled.

Opportunity is all around you. Your job is to see it, collect it, then learn how to use it for good.

PART TWO

Strategies for Seizing the Opportunities at Your Feet

CHAPTER 4

Be Positive

"A positive attitude causes a chain reaction of positive thoughts, events, and outcomes. It is a catalyst, and it sparks extraordinary results."

—WADE BOGGS

I have always said, *"A common thread among successful people is optimism."* Optimism is a critical component of achieving goals, no matter what you're facing. For example, I always felt that, regardless of the situation I was in, there was something more waiting for me, something more I could obtain, and someone more I could be. And I wanted to find that something more. I believed in a positive outcome.

It isn't always easy to be positive. Since life has a way of treating you unfairly from time to time, it can be so tempting to focus on the negatives and drown yourself in pity. But the more you practice shifting your focus to the good things you have and your road map to reach your goals, the better the outcome and the happier you will be.

Growing up in that tiny apartment in my hand-me-down clothes, I had always dreamed about having luxuries and opportunities. And I knew those dreams would come true. I *knew* I would get there. But back then, I didn't understand that, by holding that belief firmly in my heart, I would eventually reach my destination. All I knew was that there was plenty to feel happy and laugh about. And when I focused on the good that was around me, life wasn't so bad.

Indeed, finding ways to laugh has always been an important part of my mindset. That's why people say that "laughter is the best medicine." Although wealthier individuals may have been able to surround themselves with more things, in the moments when I was laughing, they were no richer than I was. The joy I felt had nothing to do with my bank account. So long as I was laughing, I was just as rich as they were.

And as I moved from selling housewares to stereos to homes to mortgages, I came to realize the product I was selling didn't matter. What mattered was my belief that I could always find enough abundance in my life.

Regardless of the industry you're in, it makes no difference if you are a thousandaire, millionaire, or even a billionaire. The only thing that matters is that you believe in what you are doing and the "why" behind it.

· Giving thought to the reasons behind your decision to go to work each day and considering the people you care most about can mean the difference between doing work that's inspired or work that you dread. The goal of creating a better life for your children and significant other can help motivate you. Every time you walk out your front door, think about the people who are counting on you and about the life you want to lead. You will have a much better chance of attaining any goal you have your eye on, whether it be in relation to your finances, family, relationships, or whatever else it is you are dreaming of, if you begin your day with understanding your "why." I will talk more about this in Chapter 15.

Progress is happiness.

No matter what I was selling, I didn't dwell on the sales I'd lost. I didn't think about all the ways that I could fail. Instead, I saw each day as an opportunity to succeed. Little by little, I made sales, and I began to accumulate a nest egg. I read a wonderful book, *The Richest Man in Babylon* by George Clason. It's a short, easy read, but the premise is to pay yourself first. Take a portion of your earnings, say 10 percent, and put that away in savings, as the first bill that gets paid. It's great advice, and I suggest you do the same!

Natural Happiness

Why do I consider myself a happy person? It's a choice. I could either be happy for the things I have, or miserable for the things I don't have. But happiness doesn't mean being satisfied with leaving things the way they are; it means being grateful and striving to be better. It means that you default to looking at the good things. We all have bad days, and we all have events and occurrences that aggravate us, but in general, I'm optimistic. Give me a little attention, love, and food, and I'm happy—just like a puppy.

Or maybe I was engineered to be positive. Even my blood type is B POSITIVE (B+). When I found out as an adult that this was my type, I threw my head back and laughed.... "Be positive!" I can't make this shit up! Positivity is literally part of my DNA.

As I write this book and share these stories and messages with you, I do so because I want your life to be everything you want it to be.

I know that being born with an optimistic outlook on life is a blessing. It truly gives you a leg up in the world.

Some people aren't born feeling happy—that's okay. Some people have to work harder to harness the feeling of gratitude. There's nothing wrong with that. If you can see yourself in that description, I have good news for you!

You can train yourself to think positively.

There are some strategies you can use to make your belief in yourself even bigger.

Kids are a great model for when we are trying to relearn our own limitless potential. They're groomed by limitations over the years. But you can unlearn these limitations. You *can* go back to that formative place and choose a different mindset.

Here are some strategies that can help you relearn the optimism that comes so naturally to children:

Practice looking at the big picture.

We are all guilty of getting overwhelmed when focusing on a challenge or unpleasant circumstance.

When that happens, it's more important than ever to gain perspective and literally count the blessings or good things in your life. While things can always be better, they can always be so much worse. Take a look around you, and you'll see those less fortunate. You'll see those who would give almost anything to gladly have *your problems.*

Then look at all the amazing things that you have: that fresh cup of coffee in your kitchen or a job to go to. There are people in places much darker than yours who would cherish what you take for granted.

Take the time to discover thankfulness and appreciation. It's very easy to take things for granted until they're gone. If you can appreciate what you have, life looks so much better.

Even though I know this to be true, I have to constantly remind myself to take a step back and appreciate all the good as well.

I often tell myself, "It's not that I *have* to do this. It's that I *get* the opportunity to do this."

Interrupt your patterns.

We are creatures of habit. We do the same things over and over, often without thinking. In fact, the vast majority of the thoughts we have each day are repetitive. If your thoughts are trending negative, you'll be wallowing in your perceived inabilities before lunch. Even if you can push through and work hard despite that negativity, you're still spending precious extra energy to cut through the resistance.

While I definitely understand the struggle, unnecessary struggle doesn't serve you. Don't go out of your way to create problems. Do yourself a favor and short-circuit negative, often unconscious patterns. It's hard to realize that your thought process becomes habitual, and we have to stop this process from occurring. If you agree with me that mindset is important, then a healthy, optimistic mindset will help you achieve a lot more than a troubled one.

That doesn't mean that there aren't obstacles. I get it. This is about focus. If you focus on the obstacles, you will never see the big picture. But when you focus on your goals, you can get past the obstacles you need to address along the way.

Here's an example: Go to Google Maps, as if you were getting directions. Do you start by looking at where the traffic is, or do you put in your destination? If you start with your destination and find the best path, you can deal with any potential obstacles along the way. Conversely, if you search for roads without traffic, you could have a smoother drive, but it may not take you to where you want to go. You'd be surprised at the countless number of people I come across who never get to their potential or desired destination because they are so focused on the obstacles. Make sure you break free of this pattern.

A helpful way to free yourself from focusing on the obstacles is to look at the big picture. Here's a quick exercise for you to try that a professional driver taught me. I always appreciated cars and the art of driving. Over the past several years, I would have a professional driver spend the day with me on the track, where he would help me enhance my driving skills. During one of my track lessons, my instructor told me. "If you want to be a better driver than the vast majority of those on the road, start with where your eyes are focused." Most drivers don't look much farther ahead than the vehicle in front of them, but well-trained drivers look much farther down the road.

Try the following exercise, and it may just make you a better driver. Take a bottle of water and place it on the ground, outdoors, about twenty feet in front of you (six or seven long steps). Now focus on the bottle. It's pretty hard to see what's happening down the road. But if you fix your eyes on the road ahead, I bet you can still see the bottle in your field of vision while also seeing the entire road in front of you. Do this when behind the wheel, and your driving skills will improve significantly. Do this in life, and success will come to you more easily.

Set time limits for dealing with hardships.

Sometimes things suck so badly that no amount of positive thinking can pull you out of the colliding emotions of devastation or loss. Life is like that for all of us, even for those who seem to bounce when they walk and send out the vibe to the world that their existence is perfect and glorious. When things suck, you need to be honest with yourself about it. Acknowledge the hardship and give yourself space to process it. Have a good cry. Write it in your journal. Wallow. But give yourself a defined yet limited amount of time to feel your feelings. Then move on. Remember, your mindset is a choice.

Complain constructively. Don't piss and moan.

Complaining is part of human nature. Unfortunately, it can also be very unproductive. Not only does complaining fail to change whatever you're complaining about, it also increases stress on your body as well as stress to the listener. I'm sure you've heard the saying, "Misery loves company," but think about how you feel when someone is complaining to you. Unnecessary complaining is not only detrimental to your mindset; it's contagious and brings down others. You literally change the energy and vibrations between each other.

But sometimes, when things aren't right, you do need to speak up. Instead of pissing and moaning, though, offer constructive advice for change, and make sure that your advice is well thought out. Be empathetic to how difficult that change might be and come up with alternatives that can be realistically implemented. You'll keep an air of positivity in the dialogue while still being considerate in your approach. Don't assume you know it all or have all the answers, because there may be holes in your solution that haven't been plugged. You will be more successful if you deliver your thoughts respectfully and positively while, at the same time, offering solutions. You may actually get the other party rooting for you and wanting to help you.

Search for gratitude.

Setbacks are inevitable, but they don't need to hold you back. They can actually propel you forward.

One way to process setbacks is to actively search for the things you're grateful for. Not only does this trick shift your perspective, but it actually rewires your brain. In the same way that your brain facilitates complaining, it can also facilitate gratitude. Use that to your advantage and practice searching for gratitude.

Some people use a gratitude journal and intentionally write down what they are grateful for each day. Others set a specific time of day to acknowledge what it is they are grateful for. What works best for me personally is, right after my first cup of coffee, to take just a few minutes to acknowledge all of the things and people I am grateful for and fortunate to have in my life. I actually say the things and names of the people I am thankful for out loud. It puts me in the right mindset because I know the obstacles that I'll come across throughout the day aren't quite that bad compared to all of the good things I have going for me. Try it. You may initially feel silly speaking out loud, but I believe it will help you keep the things that you are thankful for top-of-mind.

While the benefits are great for me, as I'm sure they will be for you, there is a much bigger ripple effect. When there is a feeling of gratitude in your heart, it changes the way you interact with others. You'll be surprised at how often you'll inspire them to spread kindness. They will carry those good feelings with them through their interactions with others.

Just recently, while in Bermuda, I was FaceTiming with my editor, Hilary Jastram, while working on this very book. I was in the concierge lounge at the Fairmount, a place I have stayed many times before. While we were talking, Pascal and Rolly, two of the servers who handle the lounge (and have done so since I can remember), presented me with a gift. They had no other reason than to thank me for how kindly I have always treated them.

When they noticed that I was FaceTiming with Hilary, they felt obligated to tell her how well I had treated them. Pascal went on to say that my treatment had actually changed his perspective. When he would go back to his native country of India, he became the guest being attended to by other servers. But his whole attitude had changed, and he treated those servers with much more kindness and respect and looked at them as friends and equals instead of as servers. Hilary said that we should put the story in the book because it was such a beautiful illustration of how the ripple effect of kindness works.

This should not be a one-time or once-in-a-while event; this should be an "all the time" thing. It's important to be kind to everyone, always, and not just to people you hope will be able to benefit you in the future. I've always felt that you can judge someone's character by how they treat a person who can't possibly do anything for them in return. People truly appreciate kindness and respectful treatment.

To give another example, I'm a big Yankees fan, and I've been a season ticket holder for many years. It seems like almost everyone who works at the stadium knows me by name because of the friendly and respectful way I treat them. Taking just a little bit of extra time to get to know them or ask them a personal question like "How's your family doing?"—and really listening to the answer—can totally change that relationship from superficial to personal. You will always be looked at as their friend. Even the bathroom attendant, Francisco, is someone I treat with the utmost respect and kindness. You can actually see him light up the moment he notices I'm at the stadium. That feeling that we get from knowing that we've made others happy is impossible to put a dollar value on.

Surround yourself with positive people.

Just as your own negative self-talk can bring you down, so can the negative talk of others. We all know how easy it is to cave to the temptation of talking badly about someone who isn't there.

Just as you can get sucked into negative peer pressure, the same can happen with positive peer pressure.

What if, instead of hearing people around you speaking negatively, you heard them speak proudly of their company? Kindly of their clients? Highly of friends and coworkers?

It's wonderful to hear them talk nicely about others who are not there. You can't help but feel how contagious it is. The positive energy fills you. While negativity may feel tempting for the moment, it always drains you in the end.

You're not always around when other people are speaking about you, and the way they talk about others will eventually be the way they speak about you. It's much better to surround yourself with people who you know will speak kindly of you even when you are not there.

Surround yourself with positive people, and you will have to do less work to push out the thoughts that stop your aspirations in their tracks. Seek out people who are following their own dreams. They will encourage you to do better rather than encouraging you to complain. The power of being around others who feel a sense of gratitude and positivity is exponential. I'm sure you have experienced how these good feelings spread as they gain more energy and momentum. And you can't help but feel a natural high as you are able to look toward the future with more optimism. In doing so, you'll be surprised at the paths that will open themselves up to you.

CHAPTER 5

Map Your Dreams

"Make no little plans; they have no magic to stir men's blood, and probably themselves will not be realized. Make big plans; aim high in hope and work, remembering that a noble, logical diagram once recorded will never die, but long after we are gone be a living thing, asserting itself with ever-growing insistency."

—DANIEL BURNHAM

I've always had big dreams. I remember wanting to be the player who saved the day, making the shot with one second left in the game. I fantasized about the bases being loaded in the bottom of the ninth and hitting that grand slam. It wasn't enough to complete the task. I wanted to complete the task when it was needed the most.

But wanting to save the day is a dream, not a plan. "Save the day" doesn't tell me where I'm going.

Let me explain what I mean. If I want to hit that home run, I need to learn to play baseball, practice consistently, get on a team, and have the chance to be up at-bat. I need a road map to get there, or I'll wander around lost, waiting for an opportunity to save the day that will never come.

I see this in finance all the time. Everyone wants to retire comfortably, yet 45 percent of people over fifty have no retirement savings at all. The median household savings, including retirement savings, is barely above $35,000...that means half of all households have less than that amount saved.

So how do we make the financial dream of retiring comfortably come true? How do we make any dream come true, for that matter?

It's important to dream it because you need to visualize it and set that goal firmly in your mind. But you need to do more than just dream.

Make a Plan

Don't just set goals. Figure out how to achieve them. The key is to *reverse engineer* every dream. Every goal that I want to attain is reverse engineered, meaning that I start with the destination and then map out the tasks in bite-sized steps.

Again, using GPS as an example, you begin your journey by first entering your destination. It's almost never a straight shot there because of the many turns along the way. Each of those segments is part of the trip. They're all mapped out, literally, to get you there. Achieving your financial or personal goals needs to be mapped out the same way, so you can find your money in the streets. It's not just "Here's where I want to go," but here's all of the required steps or segments needed to get there. Take each step toward your goal one at a time, just like you would if you were following directions on the GPS. The big difference is that Google Maps can't tell you what steps you need to take. You have to do the work or find those who can help you map the road ahead.

For example: if you want to retire at sixty, it's great to set that as a goal, but now you need to map it out. First, figure out how much money you will need each year to live off of when you're no longer working. Then think about what sources may still be available to provide you with monthly income, like Social Security. Maybe you have saved a nest egg to generate interest or payments, or perhaps you have equity in real estate that you can draw on. This will give you the total monthly income you can expect to receive without working during retirement.

Next, determine how much additional income you will need above the amount you can already expect to receive.

Then calculate the amount you need to accumulate to provide yourself with that additional income. Lastly, figure out how much you need to start periodically saving today to reach that total. It might look something like this:

You want to retire at sixty. You are currently forty, so you have twenty years to reach your goal.

You want a monthly income of $7,000 when you retire without having to work.

Social Security will provide $2,800 per month, so you are short $4,200 per month.

Assuming a 5 percent rate of return, you will need a total lump sum of $1,008,000 to generate the $4,200 per month you need. Yes, you read that right...$1,008,000 x 5% = $50,400 per year or $4,200 per month.

If you currently have $80,000 saved today, it should grow to $212,000 in twenty years at that 5 percent rate of interest.

This means that you will need to accumulate a nest egg of $796,000 in twenty years.

You will need to save $1,950 per month, every month, to reach your goal—starting today.

You can, therefore, see why it is so important to reverse engineer your plan. Remember, you can adjust your plan by, say, working during retirement. You can also use the equity you've gained in real estate or other resources that you may have. And you don't have to do this alone. A financial advisor can give you the guidance to bring your road map to life.

And it's not just finances we're talking about. It could be your career, education, or whatever it is you're trying to achieve...reverse engineer it and map it out, step by step.

Take Action

Even the best plan and well-designed road map won't get you there unless you take action.

In many years of being a professional speaker, I've gotten to share the stage with some incredible personalities. One of those was Mark Allen, a six-time triathlon winner and an accomplished speaker. But it wasn't always easy for him. He was a great endurance runner and cyclist, but he was not yet a terrific swimmer. He watched every video and read every book he could on how to improve his swimming. Mark's coach eventually had enough and said to him, "You know, at some point, you actually have to get in the water." And that's what taking action is about—getting into the water. Doing it instead of talking about it. I see this as one of the most transformational steps to take. And don't wait until it's perfect. When you feel you can add value, go for it!

Recalculate

Okay, let's go back to the GPS again.

Consider how your GPS recalculates when you encounter traffic, accidents, or closed roads, and most importantly when you miss your turn. You have to do that with your life too. Periodically evaluate your path. Are you reaching your goals at the pace you had planned? Are you realizing that where you're heading isn't what you had expected? I'm not suggesting that you throw in the towel, but eventually, you should consider recalculating the route.

In my life, I'm constantly recalculating to figure out how I can reach my goals. I'm taking into consideration what I'm learning and the ever-changing environment around me. It's always important to measure where you are, not just at the end of a task, but also as you go.

Remember my dream of hitting the game-winning home run? Well, unfortunately, that wasn't in the cards for me, at least as far as sports go. In high school, I was a good athlete. But in college, I noticed that other kids got a lot better than I did at the next level. And while I wasn't bad, I just wasn't good enough to make the team. And believe me, it was not for lack of trying. Being early to practice, staying late, and doing about all I could just wasn't enough. God has blessed me in so many ways, but not enough athletically to make the college team.

That's the thing about athletics. It isn't always fair. Those with the most God-given talent and who are willing to work at it will make the team. But that's also the great thing about sales. It doesn't matter if someone else can run faster, jump higher, or is stronger. It's just about one thing: heart. You can reach any goal by doing the work and putting in the effort. So ask yourself, *how bad do I want it?*

When I realized that sports wouldn't make my dreams come true, I changed my trajectory. That allowed me to find and focus on new opportunities that could give me the achievement and fulfillment I wanted through a different path.

Of course, you don't only recalculate because of mistakes or disappointments. You change your path because new roads open up before you. When my twins were born, I recalculated and wrote mortgages. I had to do that because my family depended on me.

It's a beautiful thing to have big dreams, but to make them come true, you must map them out. Mapping your dreams means figuring out what you want, *constructing a realistic plan to get there, taking action, and then making adjustments along the way.*

With the right plan and road map, you *can* achieve anything you desire. But with the right plan, road map, and your maximum effort in taking action, you *will* achieve anything you desire.

CHAPTER 6

Recognize Opportunity

"A pessimist sees the difficulty in every opportunity; an optimist sees the opportunity in every difficulty."

—WINSTON CHURCHILL

Most of the time, opportunity isn't going to take the shape of a pretty box that falls into your lap. It won't include a card taped to the top with your name on it, signed "Love Always, the Universe." Sure, that kinda happens every once in a while. But most of us have to learn to see the possibilities right in front of our faces. And there are so many within reach, just like the money in the streets.

Early on in my mortgage career, I tried to build relationships with unconventional sources of business. I figured that the businesses where I was the customer had their own customers who could benefit from my services. And when I was paying for the business or services they gave me, I had their attention. That's when I made sure to tell them what I did and how I could help their other clients. After all, they were my captive audience for a few minutes.

Some examples of these business relationships were my accountant, my dentist, the local pizza shop, and my haircutter, Dennis Francese. (Dennis has been one of my best friends for more than thirty years and is one of the sweetest guys on the planet. He's also one of my bandmates and a very talented percussionist.) These connections became huge sources of referrals for me that helped my business grow rapidly. Think about it, when you are getting your hair cut, the haircutter will almost always ask, "So, what's new with you?" Well, if the person getting their hair cut responded by talking about a home they were buying, then Dennis would hand my business cards to potential clients.

I received an incredible amount of business from places no one else was looking, even though they all had the same opportunities right in front of them.

Living in New Jersey means that driving along the highway requires the payment of many tolls. And while we have the ability today to make an automated payment as you drive past the booth, it wasn't always that way. Back in the days when I started doing mortgages and would travel along the highway, you could go the faster route of having exact change, or you could go the longer route and wait in a line where a toll attendant would take your cash and give you the change.

Remember my philosophy of talking to as many people as I could, especially those I was giving money to, and viewing them as potential customers? Well, even though I almost always had exact change, I took the longer route and waited in line so I could speak to the toll attendant and, along with the cash, give him or her my business card. I caught so much flack for this from my friends and others who had to tolerate the slowdown several times along the ride. But one day, a toll attendant I gave my card to, Steve Horton, called me about refinancing his loan. I did not only Steve's loan but also the loans of seventeen other toll collectors who Steve wound up talking to. Now, I'm obviously not the only mortgage salesperson who rode the New Jersey highways and paid tolls, but I tried to see things a bit differently by searching for less obvious opportunities, even though those opportunities were right in front of me and everyone else.

I picked up the money in the streets while everyone else drove on by.

Trust Your Gut

Recognizing opportunities and taking action requires a leap of faith in yourself. I see so many people miss great opportunities because they talk themselves out of moving forward. First of all, not doing anything is the easiest thing to do. It's easy to pass on an opportunity, and it doesn't require hard work, but you might regret not doing the hard work later.

We can avoid talking ourselves out of wonderful opportunities by trusting our gut, trusting what we feel inside. So often, we just know when something is right or wrong. So don't discard an idea that feels right to you just because you are afraid. If you believe in it, push yourself past the fear and go after your goal—but you must commit to it. If you pursue your dreams tentatively, with less than full effort and commitment, your chances of success will decline precipitously. Maximum effort will maximize your chances of success. Stay focused on the big picture and the enormous rewards.

There's a big decision to be made here. If you feel like you're putting things off, are you doing it because your gut is telling you to, or because you're lazy? Take the time to decide which of the two it is and either move on or over-come your laziness.

Don't make decisions that make you feel sick. I've seen people look only at a spreadsheet and projections and go for it when their gut says no. Projections don't mean anything if nobody wants the product.

So ask yourself: *would I buy this?* So many people forget that nothing happens until a sale is made. A huge key to being successful in business is to always look at a business from the point of sale, and then reverse engineer it to profitability.

One of the all-time greats at understanding this simple truth was Peter Lynch. Peter was the legendary manager of the Fidelity Magellan Fund. He racked up incredibly successful investments within the fund and created enormous wealth for his clients. Perhaps most impressively, Peter stood the test of time. He succeeded consistently for very long stretches. What was his secret? Taking it back down to the point of sale and remembering that nothing happens until a sale is made.

Peter would troll the shopping malls and look at where the kids were buying. His investment in The Gap (it's out of favor now but used to be super-hot in the '80s) returned over 800 percent. There are many other examples, too, but my favorite is the one Peter tells about how his wife always had a hard time with pantyhose. Even the most expensive ones failed to meet her expectations until she came across

L'eggs. Despite being cheaper than other brands, their performance got rave reviews from Mrs. Lynch. Peter trusted his gut, recognized the value in the company by looking at the point of sale, took action, and seized the opportunity that was before him. His investment in L'eggs rewarded him, his fund, and his investors with an 1100 percent return. That's $11 dollars back for each $1 invested.

Dealing with Risk

Of course, we need to talk about risk. No opportunity is foolproof. There's always an element of risk. That means that risk assessment should be a critical part of your process when deciding whether to pursue a product or work with a client. Everybody has their own risk threshold or tolerance. Do you know yours?

If not, don't worry! We are going to discuss this very subject.

Risk tolerance has two components: emotional and financial. Emotional risk tolerance has to do with your ability to handle failure or the prospect of it. Are you comfortable with uncertainty? Will you lose sleep—or more importantly, peace of mind—if things don't work out? Will it put stress on good relationships that you've built with others, who may be at odds with you if the business fails? Only you can answer the level of emotional capital you are willing to risk. I emphasize this not because I want to scare you, but because I want to make sure you understand that you need to be motivated and committed to the success of your endeavor. There's more than just money at stake.

And speaking of the money at stake, there are real financial risks to consider.

Can you recover financially if an investment goes wrong? What will happen if you lose everything that you put in? What is the likelihood of success or failure? The more reserve assets you have, the more financially risk-tolerant you are likely to be.

There are always success stories about people risking it all to pursue their dreams. Did you know that Sylvester Stallone was broke and turned down hundreds of thousands of dollars in the 1970s because the director would not allow him to play the starring role in the screenplay he had written, called *Rocky*? He was broke. How broke? He actually had to sell his dog, Butkus. A director eventually agreed, but Stallone had to work for the minimum allowable pay and sold the script for a tiny fraction of what he could have received. But he did great, became a star, and the rest is history. Stallone later bought back the dog and put him in two films.

While this story is inspiring and heartwarming, there comes a time when the risks are too great. Sometimes when the risks are so great that you can't afford to lose, you might not be able to afford to win.

Tolerance of any kind is best built over time. Remember when you couldn't even finish a beer without feeling sick the next day? Remember when you couldn't do a single push-up? But over time, with repetition and practice, you can build up to doing fifty push-ups. I hope you can't drink fifty beers, but you see where I'm going with this. Start small when it comes to risk.

The next step is to build on your wins and push the limits even more on your risk tolerance. Once you do this, you can target bigger and bigger projects on the way to achieving your goals.

CHAPTER 7

Amplify Your Message and Become Magnetic

"It takes the same amount of time and effort
to speak to an audience of one person or 50 people,
but the rewards of speaking to those 50 people
are much greater."

—BARRY HABIB

As a mortgage professional, I excelled at talking to one person at a time. Then I realized that I could amplify my message by talking to groups. Instead of trying to connect with just one person, why not try connecting with thirty people at a time? I made exponentially more connections and referrals once I decided to scale my communication.

Writing was also a powerful way to broaden my reach. The media is always looking for fresh meat, and I was thrilled to provide it. Questions my clients repeatedly had for me became a great source of content. I would write about how to solve these common concerns and use them to become a valuable resource for the media. This amplification was like striking gold. And today, thanks to social media, it's much easier.

You need to make yourself famous so that your reputation precedes you. Potential referral sources will be more welcoming to you. And your clients will be more eager to deal with you and less desirous of trying to negotiate. It's like magic when you position yourself as the expert or the advisor. And speaking is a great place to start.

But if you're going to speak in front of a group, you'd better have something of value to say. I had to find topics that a particular audience needed to hear and explain them in ways that made sense. Writing helped me sharpen my skills because it's much harder to write than to speak. You don't have the benefit of voice inflection in writing.

Amplifying your message through writing and using traditional or social media will greatly increase and accelerate notoriety. As a result, people will be more receptive to meeting with you and listening to what you have to say. And providing meaningful insights that add value to your audience will make you memorable. Keeping your audience engaged, however, requires you to be magnetic.

Now, everyone wants to be magnetic; we often look at others with admiration and say, "Man, that person is just so magnetic!" I've got good news for you, though. I'm about to tell you the secret of being magnetic, and it's really simple. Here's the secret:

Make everyone you come in contact with feel smarter and better, and you will be magnetic. Give them value that makes them feel smarter because of the useful insights you shared with them. Encourage and inspire them to feel better about themselves with your positivity, and they will crave more of that. They will be drawn to you, which is the definition of being magnetic.

While the trick is simple, what you provide can't be empty. You can't give what you don't have. But if you've put in the time, if you do the research and the work to find meaningful insights and solutions to share along with genuine empathy and concern for others' well-being— you're well on your way to being magnetic.

My goal has always been to improve the lives of those with whom I come into contact.

I began writing and publishing locally. And while it took time and hard work, I massively enjoyed the results!

After reading some of my published material, the local news channel—News 12 New Jersey—invited me to do a segment on camera. Even though it was a small station, it was a big opportunity. I could reach so many more people in front of the camera. But, while I knew this was an enormous opportunity, I was also terrified. Here's where risk assessment and courage came into play. I knew I was far from perfect, but I thought that I could add value, so my decision was to take action and do it.

It turned out okay.

I continued to write and publish and appear on local news programs. And all the while, I was evolving as a mortgage professional. Those smaller opportunities laid the groundwork for a really big one. If I hadn't taken all those other steps, I would have never gotten the chance I'm going to tell you about in a second. Doing all the hard work put me in a position to get lucky.

Bob Pisani from CNBC read a story I had published on an innovative way I was helping people refinance their mortgage—what I called a "zero-cost loan." I would explain to clients that their new interest rate would be lower than their current rate, but that it would be slightly higher than the lowest rates available. In exchange, their closing costs would be paid for.

This was unheard of and misunderstood. I was not adding their closing costs to the loan balance. Instead, I got the lender to pay for the client's closing costs because they were receiving a higher interest rate. Doing this was highly beneficial to the client because they didn't have to evaluate the cost versus savings and figure out how long it would take to break even. Because there were no closing costs, the break-even period was immediate, and clients started profiting right away! It was like getting money in your mailbox every month.

Bob Pisani became very intrigued by this, and he asked me to come on CNBC's show *Money Talk*, which he co-hosted with Ted David and which aired in the evenings. I was already pretty scared about being on national TV, but what was even more intimidating was that viewers could call in with questions. It's no wonder, then, that given the unknown element of having to answer questions on the fly, I was literally shaking and breathing faster and faster as the on-air countdown began. "5, 4, 3, 2, 1...you're live!"

My refinancing idea made the phone lines light up. And I became more relaxed as I forgot about the cameras and just focused on answering the questions. God must've been watching out for me because one of the callers was a woman who asked for my advice on how she could reduce her debt burden. I somehow did the math in my head and restructured all of her debts in such a way that she could save hundreds of dollars per month while also reducing the term of her mortgage by eight years. All this on live TV! Being on live TV can be quite the adventure; things can go wrong, and you have to adapt. I can recall one time while I was on the set of CNBC, my chair suddenly dropped all the way down. I did the full a six-minute segment stretching my body so my head would be in the frame of the camera.

The call-in viewer whose debts I restructured was so thrilled with the guidance I gave her that she wrote CNBC a letter stating how I had made a big difference in her life. But her reaching back out to CNBC wound up making a big difference in *my* life as well. CNBC called me back for another show, and another one after that, and so it went.

Soon I had a regular spot on CNBC that lasted for thirteen years. Then CNN, NBC, FOX, and Bloomberg came knocking. The more I helped people, the more my reach grew organically. It all started with that one show.

What luck to have Bob Pisani reading what I had published, the woman calling in, and everything falling into place just right. But while there had certainly been an element of luck to all of it, I would never have had the opportunity to experience that luck if I hadn't done all the hard work up to that point. That hard work enabled me to offer something of value, which, in turn, drew others to me.... I was becoming magnetic.

And my luck kept getting better.

I leveraged my television presence at an event with Debra Jones, who was an impactful, charismatic national speaker in the mortgage industry. I always highly valued and prioritized learning—always wanting to get better. So I went to an event where Debra was speaking in New Jersey. She was this tiny ball of energy—she talked fast, walked fast, bounced around the room, and spouted one idea after another. It was hard to take notes or follow her with my eyes.

After she spoke, I walked up to her to say hi, introduce myself, and mention how much I enjoyed her talk. Almost every speaker loves to hear that they had an impact on people in the audience.... I sure do.

As we began to chat, she said she had seen me on TV. She asked if I had done any public speaking. I told her I had, but only locally, on a small scale, to realtor offices.

With a line of people behind me, we both felt pressured to wrap it up. She smiled, pointed off to the side of the room, and said, "Please, wait." So I waited.

When the line cleared, she came to me and said, "I have an idea for you." She wanted me to call her the following week. I was so anxious about making that call, but it turned out to be a very important one that changed the trajectory of my life. Debra had a stable of speakers who she would send out to do events. She took a cut in exchange for her team handling everything from lining up the engagement to bringing in the attendees. But if you were going to be one of Debra's speakers, you had better be good at it. There's a big difference between offering free insights, which is what I had been doing, and being paid to speak. The audience expects much more from you when they are paying. I was still pretty young at thirty-two, and I had never been paid to speak. As luck would have it, Debra had just parted ways with her top speaker, Greg Frost, and was looking for a replacement. Greg was a legend at the time, so his shoes were very big to fill, but I wanted this opportunity. Although I was very scared, I pushed myself to take the chance.

Debra invited me to Claremore, Oklahoma, to attend her speaker camp, and that's how I launched my speaking career.

She taught me so many things and pushed me to have my own product. At that time, when speakers had a product to sell at the back of the room, it was usually cassette tapes—yeah, I know, my age is showing here. I took her advice, worked hard to write out all of my content, went to a studio, recorded the tapes, had them edited, got the artwork and packaging, and created a nice-looking product to sell. I was so proud of my work and couldn't wait to show Debra.

I overnighted her a sample of the final product and couldn't wait to get her feedback. Finally, she called, and I could tell she was very pleased and proud of her young protégé by her kind words and the tone of her voice.

Then she gave me some incredible advice: "Just remember that you get better; your tapes don't."

Wow.

I didn't quite understand it then, but this was truly a life lesson. It wasn't just that I would cringe at listening to those same tapes a couple of years later because I had become so much more skilled; it was much deeper.

If we wait to do something until we get better, we will never do it.

I needed to make that product to gain experience. That way, I *could* get better...and draw upon it in the future. Doing this allowed me to build toward bigger projects.

And it's been like this my entire life: selling stereos out of my trunk seems like a small step now, but that led to bigger and bigger opportunities. I owe Debra for having given me that first chance to become a professional speaker. As for Greg Frost—well, we became, and still are, great friends.

It's great for me to share these stories that worked out well. Hard work and luck—there is a connection. But I also think it's important to share our losses, and there have been many.

We talk about our wins so much more than our losses. But we do ourselves no good if we gloss over our reality and the setbacks that forge our integrity.

That's what the next chapter is about: making mistakes. But before you turn the page, take heart. Those mistakes often give you the precise information you need to succeed.

CHAPTER 8

Make Mistakes: Let Them Make You Better

"Failure is simply the opportunity to begin again, this time more intelligently."

—HENRY FORD

Most people aren't very excited at the prospect of making mistakes, but I promise you that it's necessary. You'll never get better without sucking. Learning from our mistakes is like paying school tuition. You pay to learn.

There's no such thing as a successful person who has never made a mistake. It's that simple. So if you want to be successful, you need to make mistakes. And you can't stop there. Success comes from benefiting from failures. You have to learn from them and let them make you better.

Some of my mistakes, for example, led to marriages that ended in divorce. The women were amazing, so I accept responsibility for the mistakes I made that contributed to the end of my marriages. Being able to first realize and examine my share of mistakes has helped me grow. Ultimately, by taking honest ownership of my shortcomings, I can be better in the future.

I still have wonderful relationships with them. We've even spent a few Thanksgivings together. But the greatest blessings that came from these marriages were my incredible children. If I'd have let the first failure keep me from ever trying again, I wouldn't have my two youngest sons and twenty-five great years with their mother, Toni. And I sure wouldn't be who I am today.

I am blessed by all these experiences and what they have taught me. I failed when I didn't take the time to focus on one of the most important relationships in my life. As a result, I've learned that I need to be more present. To be perfectly honest, I'm still working on this. But at least I know what I need to be aware of.

I've also made plenty of mistakes in my professional life.

One of those mistakes, one I still think about, happened at the launch of my speaking career at Debra Jones' speaker's camp in Oklahoma, which is one of the cornerstones of her program. There, I learned a lot about speaking—but I learned even more about myself.

I was the new kid on the block and had always been very competitive. *But I didn't realize just how insecure I was and how that insecurity would lead to making mistakes I would regret for a long time.*

The other speakers were quite seasoned and could have taught me through their experiences. I should have gained from their wisdom, but rather than learning from them; I tried to outdo and outshine them. Instead of taking in what they were saying, which would have helped me, I tried to be better than they were. I should have worked on building strong friendships with them instead of viewing them as a threat. I should have been open and welcoming in my interactions with the other speakers, but there was an edginess and, to some extent, even tension. When I spoke with them, I often felt the need to point out an accomplishment or something important that I was working on. My insecurities caused me to want to make that known.

And when I pointed out my accomplishments, it left me feeling unfulfilled, primarily because I was acting in conflict with my own principles. I let the fear of not being good enough, and the need to prove myself get in the way of building relationships that would have led to a much happier state of mind. I didn't realize that, as a beginner, I was there to learn and that it was okay to fail. Instead, I failed to learn.

I'm embarrassed to talk about that time, but I feel grateful for how far I've come.

As it would turn out, years later, my paths crossed with many of the speakers who had been at speaker camp. But this time, the interactions were much warmer. I was now able to appreciate how exceptional these individuals truly were. I felt this pain in my heart for actions that I was not proud of. I couldn't help but say to myself, *why were you so insecure? And why did you behave that way back then?* I can't turn back the clock, but I can continue to learn from my mistakes for future interactions.

Each failure can be turned into an investment in learning to be better tomorrow.

Here's how to suck and get better: try, suck, reflect and learn, and try again.

Try

Nobody comes out of the womb as an expert in any area. The skills they've acquired were all learned. Think about when you first started driving and how difficult it was. It seemed like there was a lot to keep track of. But over time, as you learned, it became easier and easier. The key is to try to learn new skills and to stick with it until it becomes second nature.

Suck (But Learn from It)

Nobody likes to fail. It feels bad, it's embarrassing, and there can be very real and serious consequences. The most tangible risks in business are losing money and letting people down.

However, there are other less tangible risks; for example, your confidence and self-worth can be eroded. Many people feel ashamed of their failures, and humans are not good at dealing with shame. Confidence is a fragile thing, so you need to protect yours. Find a way to turn these times where you've not been your best self into a lesson, and I promise you that you will feel much better about yourself the next time a similar circumstance arises.

It's easier to be okay with sucking when you realize that your mistakes mean you *did something wrong*, not that there's *something wrong with you*. Mistakes will happen. While we try to avoid them as best we can, they're an important part of the process...as long as we learn from them.

Reflect and Learn

Make reflection a part of your process in everything you do. Trying a new business strategy? Build in time for reflection. Identify key checkpoints. Are you reaching your goals? If not, why? What does that teach you? It can be helpful to write your experiences down. But you must also identify *what went right*. After all, most failures aren't complete fiascos.

This leads us to an even bigger lesson—allowing for time to think. Thinking is something we all presume happens, and of course, in the literal sense, that's true. But I'm talking about deliberately setting aside time to do so. Set an appointment with yourself.... After all, who's more of an expert on you than you? You will be amazed at what dedicating time to work on something that's a problem or a goal that you'd like to reach will do toward solving or attaining it.

It may be just ten or fifteen minutes each day. But let yourself dream about a goal. Let yourself feel what it would be like to get there. Go through the road map in your mind of the steps you need to take. Then reverse engineer it. Or maybe spend those ten or fifteen minutes diagnosing and working on something that you're not feeling good about. You can spend that time deciding how to best direct your energy to find a solution. Remember, while sometimes these solutions or ideas might just pop into your head, they'll do so much more frequently if you actually dedicate the time.

I do this every single day, and it's my secret weapon— almost a superpower—that helps me improve and get just that much closer to achieving my goals.

Fear of Failure

Failure can inhibit your growth in two ways: as I mentioned, it can erode your confidence, and the fear of failure can keep you from trying. However, you'll never learn from failure if you never try. That's one reason so many people are stuck right where they are: their fear of failure inhibits growth.

I experienced true fear at my first paid speaking gig. My previous speaking experience was limited, and even though I had been on TV several times, it was never in front of a live, paying audience. I thought this gig was next level, and I was totally stressed.

I had been scheduled to speak in front of a group of mortgage professionals in St. Louis, Missouri. They were expecting me to be amazing, and that was stressful enough. But to make matters worse, Debra sent her tough-to-read, almost-emotionless right-hand man, Phil Temple, to watch my speech. I called him the "Stone Temple Pilot," and he was Debra's eyes and ears. I was terrified.

I was so nervous that I threw up that morning. To be honest, that was the norm every time I was about to speak for my first year. But It's amazing how far I've come after twenty-six years of speaking professionally and close to 2000 speaking engagements. I've had just about everything go wrong that could go wrong, so now I feel I can handle almost anything. All the inevitable snafus that occur hardly phase me now. Adversity teaches us how to get through. Anxiety teaches us nothing.

Only fifteen people showed up at that first event. While you might think it would be easier to speak in front of a smaller crowd, the opposite is actually true. The larger the crowd, the more energy you feel. You can actually lose yourself in the thoughts that you're sharing. But the smaller the crowd, the more personal it gets, and the more scrutinized you feel. (Imagine giving a seminar to only one person. Awkward.)

The Stone Temple Pilot was among those fifteen people I spoke to, and he judged my every word and delivery, as well as the audience's response.

I stood in front of this small audience, and a nervous smile played on my lips as I tried to engage them, looking for clues of their approval. I mistakenly took their quiet demeanor to mean that they were less engaged. But this caused me to have more anxiety and question myself, which likely made my talk less effective.

While my first speaking engagement certainly wasn't a stellar performance, it was enough to get me on my way, because I took action.

I kept speaking and practicing, and it became a passion. I trained myself to pause when I didn't know what to say instead of inserting a filler word like "um." I recorded myself and painstakingly listened to those recordings to hear all the places I needed improvement.

This turbocharged my ability to get better because I could identify where I was lacking. It's difficult to do this when you're in the heat of it all.

I have suggested the same learning approach of recording your conversations to many sales professionals. The results and improvements are nothing short of miraculous. Most people don't realize the words that come out of their own mouths and fail to see that they often don't answer the questions their clients ask until they record and then listen to their conversations. I strongly suggest you do this, taking the time to analyze your recordings. I am confident that you will see a significant improvement in the efficacy of your interactions.

Even early on, I kept asking for opportunities to speak, although I was afraid I would suck. I challenged myself every chance I could. In fact, I'm about to challenge myself again when I record my very first book—yes, the one you are holding in your hands. To this very day, I push myself to work harder and refine my skills every time I get on stage.

I think the definition of being brave is being scared but still evolving forward.

CHAPTER 9

Keep Evolving

"Mastery never stops. If you're truly a master, you're always looking for the next level. But, it's good every now and then to realize you've got a certain level of success and own it, so there's a foundation to get more momentum."

—TONY ROBBINS

There is no finish line. No living thing stays still. It's either growing or dying. If you stop growing in your profession, others will eventually begin to overtake you if *they* are growing. Not only will this lead to less financial success, it will lead to less fulfillment for you. Note that there's a big distinction between achievement and fulfillment. You can achieve goals, but that won't mean much if it doesn't give you the satisfaction of fulfillment. *And is there anything less fulfilling than dying?* So if you want more fulfillment as part of your financial success, you must continue to grow.

Even if you're good, continue to get better. Look over your shoulder; someone may be coming for what you have. This is natural in the business world. And if you think about it, you have probably accumulated much of what you have by winning against a competitor. There is no second place. In a world of competitors, you need to stay ahead.

The more experience you have, the better your chances of winning, but only if you can draw from those experiences to give you a competitive edge. Sometimes I hear people say, "I've been in the business ten years," as if their experience makes them an expert. But here's my question: *"Is it really ten years, or is it one year ten times?"* Meaning, *have you been in business for ten years, growing and expanding your knowledge as much as possible in those years, or have you lived one year ten times?*

Ask yourself: *how many seminars have I attended or courses have I taken to improve myself?* Is your technology up to date? Are you investing in yourself by using the best tools to serve your client? All of this takes time and money. It's an investment in your future. If you don't make that investment, you put yourself in a weaker position than those who are growing beyond you. Even if you met the needs of yesterday's clients, you must benefit the customer in front of you today and plan for the one you hope to have in front of you tomorrow.

Technology is trying to replace us, so we'd better pay attention. There's no shortage of venture capital funding for tech companies that have your business squarely in their sights. They are also not bashful about making bold statements to their stockholders about how confident they are in replacing individuals with tech solutions.

Remember travel agents? Younger people may have never heard of a human travel agent. To them, it's just an app on their phone. But yes, there were actually people who did those jobs; however, they failed to act as advisors. And they have become nearly obsolete, having been replaced by technology that can perform travel-related tasks faster, cheaper, and more accurately—all in the palm of one's hand.

It wasn't that long ago that investments in owning a taxi license—also known as a medallion in big metropolitan cities like New York and Chicago—were viewed as one of the best and safest investments around. I had a friend who owned hundreds of taxi medallions in big cities. He was so confident that he continued to borrow against his ever-appreciating medallion value to buy more medallions. He spent his fortune freely on himself and generously toward others.

I remember how he and other medallion owners and investors often spoke quite confidently about how taxis would never depreciate in value because big metropolitan cities were getting more and more congested, and fewer people wanted to deal with increasing traffic, making taxis a more desirable option. Those same medallion owners would cavalierly cite the scarcity and expense of parking in these markets as a reason to fearlessly invest in and leverage their medallions (by borrowing heavily against them). They saw no reason to look over their shoulders and anticipate potential vulnerabilities in their "strategy."

And so it went; they kept pouring money in and borrowing even more money out. But they never really changed their product or service because they mistakenly didn't think they needed to.

Their flawed strategy worked fine until phone apps like Uber and Lyft came on the scene. Nobody saw this revolution coming. There was no need for these tech companies to buy expensive taxis or medallions; they just leveraged the internet to match up drivers using their own cars with people needing a ride.

Medallion values dropped dramatically for investors. The value of their investment decreased to below the amount they owed against it–their investment was upside-down. Many of these investors didn't just lose money; they lost everything, including their peace of mind. It's inspiring when we hear stories of rags to riches, but it's truly sad to see riches go to rags.

Don't Get Too Comfortable with Success

Even when things are going well, I put myself in the shoes of my competition and ask, *how would I attack? What vulnerabilities can be exploited to win business away?*

A product or service that someone is offering today may appear difficult to replace with an app, but don't count on that holding true forever. Advances in technology are always evolving and are relentless in trying to take over.

That's why I don't stay comfortable even when I am enjoying success. As mentioned, I try to identify potential weaknesses from my competitor's point of view. I then formulate the best defenses to protect vulnerable areas in my business—before my competitors have a chance to attack.

Change is coming.... It may take longer than you would have thought for it to happen, but when it does, it will happen faster than you could have ever imagined.

Continuously Grow Your Business by Removing Points of Friction

Anticipate what your business needs to do so it can continuously evolve and remain relevant to your customer. One of the best and easiest ways to do this is by *removing points of friction*. Here are just a few small examples of how I've done this in the past.

I identified a huge point of friction in the mortgage industry when it came to understanding market conditions. A major problem for the mortgage salesperson and their client was that they would often be blindsided by sudden interest rate movements. A client expecting a specific interest rate during the mortgage application process might suddenly learn that the market had adversely moved. If they hadn't yet locked in a specific rate, this could result in their mortgage interest rate and monthly payment increasing significantly. But not everyone wants to lock in a rate early on because rates can also improve between the time when they apply for their mortgage and when they actually close on their loan—which would then benefit that client with a lower monthly payment for many years to come.

I decided to fix this persistent, costly problem by launching a new company called Mortgage Market Guide, which was the first of its kind. Mortgage professionals could count on us to watch the changing interest rates for them. We would analyze market conditions and alert those who subscribed to our service so they could then alert their customers (borrowers) as to the most advantageous time to lock in their mortgage rate and avoid being surprised with a sudden, adverse rate change. The result: no more getting blindsided and lots of very happy borrowers, who would go on to save tens of thousands of dollars throughout the life of their mortgage loan. This built tremendous trust between the mortgage professional and their customer. By removing this point of friction, Mortgage Market Guide experienced exponential growth and profitability, and our service became ubiquitous within the mortgage and real estate industries.

Alleviating points of friction can apply to every industry. For example, I started a medical imaging company called Healthcare Imaging Solutions. We performed high-end imaging for early cancer detection and heart disease. I hope that you personally never have to go for a scan, but if you have had experience with getting scans done in the past, you probably know that the tech conducting your scans can likely discern whether there's something serious in your images. You may even ask that tech, "How does it look?" But the tech is prohibited from telling you. You have to wait for your physician to let you know your results. That can take several days, and the anxiety can be overwhelming.

That's why, when I opened my medical imaging company, I put a radiologist right on the premises. This meant that by the time you got dressed and were headed to the consultation room, the radiologist had already reviewed your pictures and could give you an immediate diagnosis. We removed the waiting and, more importantly, the anxiety. You either got great news or had a plan for how to move forward. That practice quickly grew to three locations before I sold it.

Another example of removing points of friction happened soon after I opened *Rock of Ages* on Broadway with my partners. I noticed that patrons who wanted to enjoy an adult beverage prior to the start of the show waited in line and paid good money for their drinks. But they often arrived only a few minutes before the start of the show, and the beverage lines could be long. This meant they often got their drinks shortly before the curtain went up. Here's the problem: patrons were not allowed to take their drinks to their seats. So I witnessed them guzzle their expensive drinks and sometimes even spill them on their lovely outfits.

In an effort to alleviate this obvious point of friction, one of the other producers and I approached the theater owners and asked why we simply couldn't allow the patrons to take their drinks to their seats. The owners responded by saying, "No, we can't do it because we have never done it before." My answer was: "That doesn't seem like a good reason to me, so let's be the first to do it." It took a lot of negotiation, but *Rock of Ages* became the first show in Broadway history to allow drinking in your seat. We removed a big point of friction, and today, virtually all Broadway shows allow patrons to enjoy adult beverages in their seats during the performance, making for a much better experience.

These are just a few examples of how I removed points of friction in different industries to give clients a better experience and achieve growth for my companies. Removing points of friction can help any business, yours included. I share these examples in hopes that you will be able to more consciously look for these opportunities in business, as well as in your personal life.

Sometimes, easing a little point of friction can have enduring results that will pay dividends to you over and over. You may not want to spend the initial time to implement a process that can remove a point of friction, but you have to remember that it isn't time spent; it's time invested.

At MBS Highway, where I am the CEO, our entire culture is about getting better, providing more value, and finding ways to alleviate points of friction every day. We don't just say this; we live it.

CHAPTER 10

Building Trust and Better Relationships Through Excellent Communication

"There's a big difference between listening and
waiting for the other person to stop talking."

—BARRY HABIB

Communication is the Lifeblood of Everything

Much of the world's problems could be solved—or even better, avoided—with clearer communication. Look at the most successful people you know. Look at the best relationships you can point to. I'll bet a key to their success, and a common thread for their strength is *excellent* communication.

We must improve and refine our communication skills constantly. Your message needs to be clear, smooth, and articulate. I cannot stress enough the importance of what you just read. Sharpen your communication, and the world will reward you with more than you've ever dreamed.

One effective way to sharpen your communication skills is to get feedback on your messaging from the most novice of individuals because if they can understand your message, almost anyone can. Sure, it's fine to get feedback from experienced and reputable sources, but perhaps the most value will come from the feedback of novices. Here's the thing: you must try to forget your own expertise. The common terms, abbreviations, acronyms, and initials that you throw around, which come from your experience and familiarity, need to be discarded immediately if you are to be an effective communicator. I always use the phrase "spoon-feed your message" and recommend that you leave nothing to ambiguity.

I've had experience as an actor and film producer, and one thing I admire about some of the best content in film and entertainment is the writer's ability to give the audience a clear message that they can follow. The best authors spoon-feed the message to set up the viewer, listener, or reader for the payoff. That payoff can be in the form of a laugh, a cry, or the realization of an idea. It's much more difficult to follow along when you're constantly guessing. That may be okay for a murder-mystery movie, but it just doesn't work when you're trying to express your ideas to someone else in business or in a relationship.

Communication is so underrated and so misunderstood, yet it's perhaps the most important exchange between people that can happen.

So what is successful communication? It's taking an idea that resides within your brain and transferring it to another person's brain while making sure that they understand it. This is even more important when you're trying to reach a group of people or a larger audience. Great communicators understand how to do this. They know their ideas did not just pop into their brains. It took a path of formulation. A very common mistake is for one person to try to insert an idea into someone else's brain without the benefit of helping them understand how that formulation took place.

The recipient of an idea that is not effectively communicated may not understand it. Additionally, they may be hesitant to admit their confusion because of their pride or potential embarrassment. So they politely nod their head as if they had understood and come away with nothing. This communication failure leads to misunderstandings, as well as lost clients and sales. Master communicators don't just implant the idea into someone else; they metaphorically hold the recipient's hand through the journey of that idea. Of course, they shorten the ride to save valuable time, but nonetheless, they understand that the journey must be taken if they are to communicate effectively.

Once your message has been properly communicated, how do you influence the recipient to move forward? You do it with trust.

Trust: The Magic that Makes Things Happen

Is there anything more important than trust in a business or personal relationship?

If your client trusts you, price becomes less important. And in any relationship, trust will make each party want to give greater effort toward the relationship, leading to better results and greater longevity.

There are two important ways to build trust.

The first is with knowledge and insights. If you put in the time and effort to gain expertise, and you can effectively communicate that expertise to someone, you will begin to gain their trust. As I mentioned earlier, this is easier said than done. You must have real value to offer—something that the other party doesn't already know. Something that can, in some way, improve their life. It might be financial, time, entertainment, or life advice. And here's a secret for you: start what you're about to say with, "Do you know...?" It almost always grabs the other person's attention. Try it.

But before we get too far, let's be clear on something. Unwanted advice is often resented—just ask a teenager.

We can't just start spewing advice to others because they may get offended. *Who the heck are you to tell me what to do?* could be running through their minds. The trick is to plant the seed when the ground is fertile. Begin that process by asking questions. Just about everyone's favorite subject is themselves, so make your conversation about them. Discover where you might be able to help through questions. Then be very careful in how you proceed.

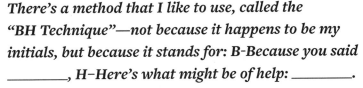

There's a method that I like to use, called the "BH Technique"—not because it happens to be my initials, but because it stands for: B-Because you said _____, H-Here's what might be of help: _____.

This is a gentle yet powerful approach to encourage someone to be more receptive to what you are about to say. It's all part of being an effective communicator. Since you've asked the other person questions and have put in the time to gain the knowledge, your advice will be relevant to the individual and provide them with insights they can use to make a positive difference in their life. Best of all, they will welcome this advice.

Here's a set of questions you can use to better understand and advise your clients, as well as build trust in your relationships:

1. What does your ideal client or relationship look like?

    This question will get them talking and help them describe the personalities they like to work with; meanwhile, you can assess if this relationship would be a good fit for you.

2. Where do you see your business or personal goals over the next five years?

    Here's where they get to dream and share their vision. Please refrain from speaking and interrupting their thought process. Make sure you take notes as to how you might be able to help them reach their goals by using the "BH Technique."

3. Tell me what you like about your current relationship?

    Their answer will give you their level of expectation based on what they're currently experiencing. Be honest with yourself in making sure you can meet their needs.

4. If you could, what would you change about your current relationship?

    Their answers might start off slow, but here's where you get the real gold, so be patient if they pause. Don't rush to fill the silence, because they may be formulating their response. And their response will tell you what's missing in their current relationship and how you may be able to win them over. Again, the "BH Technique" allows you to show them ways you can fill their needs in a targeted and non-threatening way.

Use these four questions, along with the "BH Technique" as part of your process to gain and build strong relationships.

The second way to build trust may feel counterintuitive, but it's highly effective: tell the other party all the bad stuff. Yup, you read that right. Tell them everything that's bad. We often fail to do this because we think that it will hurt our chances of success. But the truth is that this fear can sabotage the very relationship we're trying to win over. It's more powerful and limiting to our growth than most people understand.

Several years back, I learned how to juggle. I'm not that great; I'm decent at it—but I'm even prouder that I was able to show my son, Dan, how to do it because he's become an amazing juggler. When I was first taught how to juggle, my juggling instructor (yes, there are such people) made me purposely let the balls drop. My initial reaction was WTF? But he later explained that letting the balls drop is a very important part of the process. We must okay with things not working out and moving on; otherwise, we'll be too stressed to juggle. We have to get over our fear of loss.

There is an animal in South America called the spider monkey. These creatures are very difficult to capture, especially since they're both clever and nocturnal. But hunters have come up with a way to catch them that exploits their fear of loss. They leave a heavy, vented box full of the monkeys' favorite foods with only one small slit in the box as the entry point. The monkeys find the food at night because they are drawn to the intoxicating scent. Their keen intelligence allows them to find the slit quickly and grab the food, but they are then unable to extract their clenched fist with the food in-hand because it won't fit through the thin slit. The monkeys refuse to let go, allowing the hunters to simply pick them up off the jungle floor. The fear of loss—in this case of the food—endangers the animal's freedom, and they trap themselves. Human beings often fall into a similar type of trap.

When a salesperson acts needy and pushy because they're afraid of losing the sale, they appear desperate, which turns you off as the consumer. That's because your brain translates their desperation as meaning the salesperson needs to make the sale so badly, it doesn't matter whether it's in your best interest. Trust will never be built when that's the case. But when the salesperson points out all the pitfalls, putting their commission at risk to protect you, you can't help but trust them.

Think of the restaurant server who told you to avoid the meatloaf because it had been sitting, the clothing salesperson who admits that the outfit doesn't do you justice, or a salesperson who has advised you in any transaction of what to watch out for...even if it risks their sale. That kind of fearless honesty, which puts the best interests of the customer ahead of the salesperson's commission, will transform any transactional relationship to one of greater trust. The customer will perceive the salesperson as an advisor who is metaphorically sitting by their side and working with them, instead of sitting across the table negotiating against them.

And this doesn't just apply to business; when the other party is vulnerable and honest about their shortcomings, instead of putting on false airs and pretenses that they'll never live up to, your trust in them increases.

We also need to get comfortable with being the bearer of bad news, because that straightforward candor builds trust. People often avoid delivering bad news and instead go into hiding. They don't return calls or texts, which is very frustrating for the person waiting for an answer. That frustration ultimately turns into anger, and when the bad news invariably gets delivered, the circumstances only get worse. But if bad news is delivered quickly and honestly, using reliable communication, you often find that both parties will work as a team to find a resolution because they trust each other. It's not easy to deliver bad news, and the response from the person receiving it isn't always polite. But doing so will go a long way toward preserving your reputation.

It won't always be bad news that you deliver either. Many times, we get to look forward to making that call to share good news about how we pulled through for that customer. When this happens, it's often because we've drawn from our experience, expertise, and abilities—our gifts— that we have been blessed with.

Gifts are wonderful, but you must leverage them to be a better communicator.

Before my college years, I aced most tests and even skipped a grade because I was gifted with a great memory and a high aptitude for learning. But once college began, those gifts became a handicap.

When I went to college at Bernard M. Baruch College, memorizing what was taught in class wasn't enough. I remember taking those initial tests and thinking, *wait a minute! We didn't cover this!* I had never learned how to study independently.

I had a choice to make: figure it out or go home.

I chose to independently learn how to source knowledge and gain expertise in whatever I pursued—a tactic I use every day in my life.

Increasing our ability to learn independently and using our wonderful gifts magnifies our value to others—especially if we can effectively communicate our knowledge and wisdom. Remember that information is everywhere, but wisdom is a valuable commodity.

In an effort to constantly up your game, ask yourself: *am I just memorizing the concepts and strategies to run my business, or do I really know and own them?*

It's much more effective to research and understand a concept and then communicate what you've learned than it is to just memorize and parrot it back to others as I did in my earlier school years.

These types of effective communication strategies will assist you in building greater trust and stronger relationships now and in the future.

CHAPTER 11

Don't Beat Yourself

"Eventually, you learn that the competition
is against the little voice inside you that wants
you to quit."

—GEORGE SHEEHAN, M.D.

One of the fun things I get to do as a hobby is singing in a band. It's a wonderful diversion, and I'm blessed to have bandmates who are incredibly talented and a pleasure to be around. Our lead guitar player, Brad Capinjola, is the most talented guitar player I have ever heard—and I've heard many gifted guitarists. Joe Imbesi, Dan Prestup, and Semi Quaver round out the gifted musicians I get to perform with. Our band, which I named Rock of Ages Band, is quite good. We've played some major events and, for the past three years, have been fortunate enough to be flown out to the Super Bowl to play at the huge party that happens the day before the big game. A few thousand people show up, and the attendees include many famous athletes, media personalities, and entertainment stars from both music and film. It's an awesome day.

The host of this event is Wheels Up, the premier private aviation company in the U.S. Kenny Dichter, the CEO, is a very successful businessman and one of the best marketers I have ever met—a true genius. Best of all, Kenny embodies leadership through serving others, with empathy, kindness, and humility. I consider myself blessed to call him a good friend.

Kenny has the most amazing Rolodex you can imagine. He knows all the big names, and they all love him.

Saturday morning, the day before the game, Kenny invited me to a small breakfast with Coach Bill Belichick, who would coach in the championship game the very next day. Since the Patriots have been in the championship for the past three years, Kenny has been kind enough to set this breakfast up each time and invite me to be by his side. The wisdom that Coach Belichick has shared at these breakfasts has exceeded my wildest expectations. I never anticipated receiving so many life lessons during the time spent with him.

I'd like to share a few of the many lessons that I took from those meetings.

Once, when we were having breakfast, someone meant to throw out a compliment to Coach Belichick by saying, "You're so great at making adjustments for the second half of the game." I could see that Bill took this as a back-handed compliment because of the look on his face. Bill immediately responded, "If you wait until the second half to make adjustments, you're done." He continued to say, "When you prepare for a game, you can only prepare for three quarters, because what you do in the final quarter is dictated by the score and game situation. What we need to do is watch carefully for what the other team is trying to do. While there might be some initial deception involved, eventually, you'll know what that team is trying to accomplish. Maybe they're attempting to exploit one of your weaknesses or establish one of their strengths."

Whenever I'm fortunate enough to listen to Coach Belichick, I try to translate his football wisdom to business. Think about how you communicate with your clients. We often forget to listen to them and find out what it is they're trying to accomplish. We're so busy selling that it keeps us from being able to advise them. It's important to ask your clients what is meaningful about what they're trying to do.

Here's where it gets interesting. Your client's initial answer is what they *think* they might want. But remember that they probably don't have the experience to know what's best. So if you just give them what they want, you probably aren't going to stand out very much. After all, all you really did was not screw up. But if you use your wisdom and expertise to articulate what it is they truly need and could benefit most from, you've given that client an experience instead of a transaction.

Back when I was doing mortgage loans, if someone wanted to refinance their mortgage, they came to me thinking they wanted a lower rate. Sure, that seems logical, but I would look at their entire financial picture. What if we used this opportunity to pull out some of the equity from the appreciation of value in their home to reduce their other debts, like car loans and credit cards? We might be able to take some of that money to allow them to enjoy their home even more by renovating the bathroom or kitchen. It's hard to put a price on that daily enjoyment.

And then let's really change their lives by touching a hot button—they likely don't have money saved for their children's college, but I promise you, it's on their mind. There's a good chance that their retirement savings are not enough to give them the retirement they want. By restructuring their debt and saving them lots of money each month in cash flow, I would show them a strategy where they could reinvest that cash flow savings back into their mortgage. This would often result in them paying off their mortgage a dozen or so years earlier than they had planned to—all while building equity for them, sometimes in the hundreds of thousands of dollars that they could use for retirement or their kid's college. Plus, they got that upgraded bathroom.

All this would be done without making any changes to the amount of money they were paying toward their bills each month. While they thought they wanted a better rate, I helped them have a better life.

Listen to your clients carefully and stop selling. Advise them, and your business will grow exponentially because those clients will likely tell everyone they know about you.

At another breakfast with Coach Belichick the day before the big championship game against the Rams, I asked him for his thoughts about the game. He said, "We're prepared." There was a silence afterward, which Coach went on to fill by saying, "They can probably only run about sixty or so plays, but we're prepared for all three hundred in their playbook. You see, they're not going to fool us or surprise us. We've put in the time and hard work to make sure that *we are not going to beat ourselves*. We're going to do everything that we possibly can to prepare in a way that we *don't* beat ourselves. If they (the Rams) are going to win this game, they're going to have to beat us. They're going to have to be better than us...because we won't beat ourselves."

I still get chills thinking about that conversation. It's such a great lesson for anyone in sales, anyone in business, anyone aspiring to be more than they are at this moment.

If your competition beats you because they were just better, even though you've done everything to be prepared, it isn't fun. But when you lose to someone who's not better than you are, that's beating yourself. The feeling is agonizing.

Don't make it easy for others to take food off your table or money out of your pocket. Make it so that they can't take that victory from you easily. Put in the hard work and the preparation it takes to learn the advice that your clients need.

A professional boxer trains a thousand minutes for every minute in the ring. How many minutes have you trained before you pick up that phone and talk to a customer? How much work have you put in so that you've gained the expertise to be able to give the other party real value?

This lesson applies outside the world of business too. Remember what I said about being magnetic? The investment in your education, training, and practice will reward you over and over again and lead you to bigger and better achievements.

Beating yourself is preventable!

Here's one more of the many lessons from Coach Belichick: keep your ego in check. He made a comparison between two incredible future Hall-of-Fame quarterbacks, Brett Favre and Tom Brady. While many of their statistics are comparable, they have two big differences: Tom Brady has had many more Super Bowl appearances and wins, and Brett Favre has thrown many more interceptions. Coach Belichick attributes these differences to ego. Tom Brady won't force a throw in a high-risk situation because he knows the game isn't all about him. He doesn't have to be the star. If the defense gives him the run, he'll hand off the ball. If the defense gives him the short pass, he'll drop it off. Tom Brady wants to win—just win—whether or not he is getting the starring role. In doing so, he *becomes the star*.

Are you, as the offense, taking what the defense gives you to win? Are you doing the research to understand the best solutions to offer your client? Returning to that mortgage example, if the lower rate wasn't a real benefit, there's no reason to force it. What the defense gave us was home price appreciation, allowing equity extraction to be used for debt restructuring, which changed the client's life. This ties perfectly into alleviating the points of friction we previously discussed.

Whatever your business or relationship, take what the defense gives you; make the most of the situation you're in instead of trying to force something that probably won't happen. Your time will come for the big opportunity, and you'll be in a much better position to score.

Sometimes getting into position is as simple as answering your phone or returning an email immediately. That's the low-hanging fruit, so do it as a matter of course.

When I'm traveling, people don't even know I'm not in the office. I find ways to do the work and stay connected. Technology, the very thing that can put you out of business, can also drive your business forward if you use it correctly. You can take a call or answer an email anywhere. It's amazing to me how the same people who talk about time management won't pick up the phone to answer it.

It's one of the most foolish and preventable time wasters there is. We all know how hard it can be to get someone on the phone. So grab them when you have them; otherwise, you have to call them back when they may not be available, and the vicious game of tag begins. Finally, you set up a call for six days later, after the exhaustion of tag wastes the first two days.

This is the epitome of inefficiency.

Answer the damn phone! And if you're so busy that you can't, you can afford to get an assistant to manage the phone. Train and empower your assistant to be your clone, not a robot. They need to be able to handle the call, not just parrot a message. That means investing the time to train them. My assistant, Nicole Stallone, is an extension of me, and everyone knows that she can handle many situations because she has been empowered to do so. People enjoy and appreciate interacting with her because she is competent and pleasant. It makes me more efficient, and the people I interact with are much happier because I invested the time with her. There's a big difference between spending time and investing time.

CHAPTER 12

Win by Staying on Offense

"The best defense is a good offense."

—UNKNOWN

The best way to score is by being on offense, and having a plan helps us stay on offense.

The plan doesn't have to be fancy or high-tech; it just has to exist. Do you work from a list? If you don't, start right now! Get a yellow pad and a pen. Or make your list electronically, but for goodness' sake, have a list. You need to drive your day and have objectives. Otherwise, you are only playing defense on the things that come at you during the day, which makes it hard to score.

Every day, I make a list of the things I need or want to do during that day. I stay on offense by keeping to that list. Maybe it's tasks, or maybe it's calls. I just grind away. I stay on my list and score every time I knock something off. Sometimes it's a small score, but sometimes it's a big win. And sometimes, it even means hearing a "no" on a possible deal, but at least I can move on. It feels good to get things off my list; when I do that, I gain confidence and momentum. My list is monitored throughout the day—some things get done, others pushed to a later date, and more items get added.

Having a great plan includes building the right team to help you achieve your goals and participate in ideas and feedback to help your business evolve. When you have built your team and created an "idea environment," the results are like magic. Do all of that, and you'll fall in love with your business.

Build Your Team So You Can Build Your Empire

I know that the lessons in this book will bring you a lot of success. All you need to do is execute them. As you become more and more successful, you will need more help, which means you must hire people.

When I hire someone, here is what I look for:

- ▶ **Attitude:** Positive attitudes are contagious, and so are negative ones. Getting along with others, having a pleasant disposition, and wanting to take on challenges with an optimistic outlook are all extremely helpful in getting you closer to your goals and doing so in a more enjoyable environment.

- ▶ **Aptitude:** How well does the candidate learn? Can they catch on? If the answer is that they grasp things quickly and can almost finish your sentences, then you may want that person on your team.

- ▶ **Initiative:** You won't always be there to tell them what to do. Can they take action to get things done without being told? Can they assess situations and figure out what to do next? If they don't move unless you tell them to, they *will* hold you back.

- ▶ **Sense of Urgency:** Time is the only thing we can't replace. Don't you love it when someone says, "Let's knock this out right now"? What a winning attitude! A sense of urgency in people means they want to solve problems and will try to solve them NOW. Urgency tells clients, "You're important to me. Your time is valuable." Embody this in your attitude and actions, and the client whose concerns are treated with urgency will often become a repeat customer. Kicking the can down the road delays your progress as well. Win with urgency.

Notice that I don't need the candidate to have experience or a specific degree. That's because I know that if someone has those four qualities, I can teach them anything. If they have a good attitude, it will be a pleasure to teach them, and high aptitude means they will pick up what I am putting down. Initiative helps them take the next step, as their sense of urgency stops any procrastination. Together, these qualities help your hires help you reach your goals.

I wanted to get Coach Belichick's thoughts on hiring, so I asked him what he looks for in a player. He said, "Three things. They have to be smart, tough, and dependable." Coach explained that being smart has obvious value. But being tough doesn't mean just being physically tough; it means mental toughness as well. No whining, no thin skin to criticism, and having the toughness and determination to do what it takes to win. But I was surprised when he said that the most important quality of all is dependability.

Coach explained that if a teammate could depend on the person to their left and to their right, then they could be more aggressive. So simple, but so brilliant.

If you have to do part of someone else's job because they keep screwing up, that will hold you back. If you can depend on your teammates to do their job and do it well, *you* can be more aggressive. You can reach higher, accomplish more, and take your business much further much faster.

Have a great team of dependable people who do their jobs well, so you can lead them (and yourself) to higher levels.

We must also be committed to making the investment to teach the teammates we hire. It's not that easy, and it takes time, but the rewards for this investment are significant in both time and dollars.

In all the businesses I have owned, we've had a teaching and learning environment. You can't ask someone to do something without explaining why you do it, what the big picture is, what it means to the customer, and why it is important to you.

We currently have a good-sized group of IT people here at MBS Highway. They are awesome and talented. Rick Hanson is brilliant and runs this amazing team. We make sure that our entire IT team knows the specifics of how every new tool helps the client and their customer, how it does good in the world, and the advantage it gives our company. Teaching our IT team all the non-tech intel takes additional time, but it gives them a deep understanding and gets them thinking in ways they would never have otherwise. This creates superior products that are brought to market faster because the design hits or exceeds the objective.

The investment of time to teach your team will slow you down a bit at first, but before long, you will reap bigger rewards. And your employees will feel better about their work because they are growing. Growth toward fulfillment is important. And that's not the only benefit. We also share all the love and all the positive feedback we get; we share the piles of stories from our clients about how our team's contributions have helped our customers and our customers' clients. The sense of pride our employees gain is beyond measure. They are less likely to leave and more likely to push themselves to do even more for others because they see the value they bring. Fulfillment in the workplace makes for a much happier environment with less turnover.

Foster an Idea Environment

I have been blessed with strong creativity, but I can't be the only one with ideas to help my company. We encourage and empower our teammates to make suggestions that can improve our products and processes. Our head of social media, Megan Anderson, has sparked the formation of new tools our clients love. Matt Zadroga, who heads our sales team, has pointed out countless ways to tweak our tools.

Our customer service heads, Bill Hagman and Jessica Assip, don't just provide amazing client service, they take the feedback and bring it to our meetings for us to incorporate in product enhancements. Our subscribers see how willing we are to innovate, so they help us by pointing out ways for us to serve them better...and we respond by taking the good ideas and developing them. My daughter, Nicole, is a mortgage loan officer. She has given me ideas that have turned into products that help us grow. Our C-suite team, Avi Habib and Jill Boryszewski search for holes in our system and give ideas on how to fix them. My son, Dan, is my right hand and constantly works on product improvements and ways to improve my speaking presentations. There are many others, but you get the idea: if you create and foster an environment where your team wants to bring ideas to the table that help the company improve and grow, the sky is the limit.

It doesn't have to be *my* idea—I want the *best* idea.

Let's Talk About Time and Sales

The sales process can be complicated, but at its core, there are three phases where we spend our time: prospecting, selling, and following up. All three are essential, but where do you make the money? Only one of these will ring the cash register...selling. Since all three are essential, we must do them all and do them all well. But nothing happens without a sale. This is where you must focus. Try to effectively automate or delegate some of the prospectings and following up. You can jump in to be the hero or give that extra touch when it makes a high impact. But focus your time on selling. Otherwise, you will fall into the dreaded "selling wave." Meaning, you will do a bunch of business—which is great—but then your need to follow up will take away from prospecting and selling, so your sales will slow the next month. Then with fewer deals to follow up on, you focus on selling again. Your income rides this wave up and down.

Hire the right team, then effectively delegate and automate much of the prospecting and follow-up so that you can build your business.

Get People Rooting for You

You will have much more success if you get others to root for you. How do you do that? Well, if you catch a sporting event on TV, and you don't have a strong opinion about who you want to win, who do you pick to root for? The underdog! Yes, we root for the underdog. So, while we may not want our business to look like "the little engine that could," we don't have to be Mr. or Ms. Perfect either and portray ourselves with no flaws. You can put less pressure on yourself.

The best negotiation coach I knew of was Jim Camp. I am so proud that he was my friend. One of the many things he taught me was the "Columbo Effect." If you ever saw the TV show *Columbo*, you might recall that Columbo was brilliant, but he didn't let on that he was. He appeared very human because he let some of his mistakes show. This made others let their guard down and often help him... a.k.a., root for him. I often share stories of my mistakes and silly gaffes because I want my potential client to know that while I am competent and well-qualified, I'm also human. This helps them relate to me and root for me. Once people are rooting for you, it's far easier to overcome challenges.

How the Heck Did They Do That?

Looking at a successful person or company and trying to figure out how they got to their level can be overwhelming at times. Doing this may give you the impression that it is too big of a jump from where you are to reach their level of success. This is even more problematic if the person is your competition. They keep winning clients instead of you, and from the outside, it looks like they have some sort of magic going for them. You want to know how they do it.

This is one reason why I really like magic shows.

Magicians and illusionists fascinate me so much that I even co-produced *Criss Angel: Mindfreak* in Las Vegas at Planet Hollywood. It's an awesome show, and I still don't know how he does the illusions. But a few years back, I did get a rare inside look at how magic is made.

I went to a David Copperfield magic show at the State Theatre in New Brunswick, New Jersey. The show was fantastic. My brain was in overdrive trying to figure out how he did all those amazing tricks, one after another. I was in awe with my jaw dropped. Then it was time for the final trick: David Copperfield was going to make a dozen people from the audience disappear! Well, I wanted to be one of those being made to disappear so I could see how it was done.

David selected the participants by throwing out sixteen huge bouncing balls into the audience. Music started playing for the crowd of 3,000 strong. And if you were lucky enough to be holding a ball when the music stopped, you came up on stage to participate in the trick!

This was my big chance, but the odds were clearly against me—just one ball for every 187.5 people. (Yes, I actually did the math in my head; it's just how I am wired.) It was a musical chairs kinda lottery with big balls. The balls bounced as the music played loudly, and if you touched a ball while the music was still playing, you had to bounce it away. I watched a ball come so close, then another. People were looking at me, but I was like a man on a mission. Then a ball was heading toward me.... I lunged for it, bumping a few poor folks along the way (I did feel bad for a minute). But at last, I snatched that ball!

The music stopped, and I had won! I had the golden ticket! I was sooooo happy as I proudly headed toward the stage. I was finally going to see how this magic shit really happens.

There were twelve seats—but wait a minute—there were sixteen ball catchers. Something didn't add up. As we came up to the stage, David himself directed the winners to either one of the twelve seats or to a corner of the stage. I was one of the ones he told to go to a corner of the stage. I really didn't know what was up until he told the four of us on the corners that we were going to be the up-close witnesses. WHAT?! Or really, WTF?!

So, not only did I not disappear or learn anything, but now, I was totally frustrated because I saw this magic trick happen right in front of me. The twelve people seated were covered with a large tarp, and then suddenly, they were gone! It was an awesome show, but I was sort of pissed.

I quickly got over my disappointment and reflected on the enjoyment of the wonderful evening...until...a year later, when I saw promotions for the return of the show at the same location as last time.

Mark Haines was the then CNBC anchor of *Squawk Box*, where I was a regular. He was a dear friend and wanted to go. So I said, "Yeah, sure," thinking, *It will be a fun time, and maybe there will be some new illusions*. And while the performance was good, it was the same show as before, and I still hadn't a clue how any of the illusions worked.

But then came the finale...again the balls! Perhaps another chance? *But that would be crazy...another room of 3,000 with only sixteen balls. Another 1 in 187.5 chance. Is it too crazy to think I can make it happen?* Well, you know my blood type, B Positive, and you know I am the eternal optimist, so I really thought I *could* do it. I actually felt that I would catch a ball. The balls came flying! The music started blaring! My heart was racing, and I envisioned another chance.

I know it sounds crazy, but I did it! I got a ball! I may have knocked a few more people over in the process, but damn it, I had the ball, and I was headed on stage! As I proudly raced up to the stage, a feeling of great accomplishment put a huge smile on my face.

But then, as I walked up the stairs, I saw David. And do you f'ing believe he told me to stand at one of the corners??

I swear to you this is all true.

Well, if you know me by now, you know that I am not going to give up without trying. So there I was, negotiating with David Copperfield in the midst of his live show! I said, "Please, you made me do the corner thing last year. Can you please let me be in the trick?" He asked, "Are you a magician?" I said, "No! I'm in the mortgage business!"

Our eyes locked. I tilted my head and smiled at him and added, "It would mean a lot to me." I got him rooting for me. He said, "Okay!" I sat down in one of the twelve seats and got the whole behind-the-scenes dirt on how the trick is done.

So here is the lesson...once you know the trick, it's not as mystical. It's not magic. It's an investment of time, knowledge, skill, practice, and more practice. And with those elements in play, anyone can learn to do it. In business, don't ever be intimidated. Find out how they are doing it. Be resourceful; it's not impossible to learn or to catch your bouncing ball. Then work hard and practice. And practice more until you nail it.

Here's the best part...soon others will be looking at you and wondering how you did it.

Remember this: It's not magic; it's magical!

Fall in Love with Your Business

If you want to succeed, you must be in love with your business. It should have a gravitational pull that you can't ignore. It's a good thing to want to check in while you are on vacation. If you don't check in or care what's going on without you, consider that a warning sign. Your business is your baby. Love it and nurture it and it will grow to make you proud.

If you're not in love with your business, you need to figure out why. What is your business lacking? Is it even right for you?

Just remember that if you don't love your business, it just might not love you back.

PART THREE

How to Use Your Opportunities in the Service of Others

CHAPTER 13

Nurture Relationships

"If you want to be interesting, be interested."

—AUSTIN KLEON

I often say that "life is about relationships." They can make the quality of your life and enjoyment level so much better. We all want to be treated like we're special. It feels great and looks really good on us too. Everyone wants to know who that person is that is getting the extra love. People want to know you and be closer to you.

Being treated with extra love doesn't just happen. We must earn it. People have to want to treat us that way from their hearts. And the way we receive this is by being good to others and treating them with extra love, attention, and kindness. It all starts with us. We hold the keys to this. It's ridiculously easy...just be a giver! Initiate goodwill to others. Don't ask for favors...offer them. And don't get bummed because some people will be takers and not recip-rocate. Just let it go. Other people will appreciate you and want to do something nice in return to make your life and experiences better.

One of the great speakers of all time and someone who was a mentor to me, Jim Rohn, always said to "attend the gatherings." Get out there and talk to people! I do. I work the room at events and interact with people I don't yet know. Make sure you strike up conversations, get people's contact information to follow up, make kind offers of ways you can help them, and don't just chat with the person you came with or the people you already know; make new con-tacts, relationships, and friends.

Network!

Make introductions to others who can benefit from connecting. Then you will become the go-to person who can put people in touch with someone who can help them. Because you have grown your network and can match people up, they will be more inclined to refer you as well. But they'll also be more inclined to consider you a friend. And while there are many ways that you can benefit financially, it gets even better. It will enrich your life experiences because many people in your network can introduce you to people in *their* network who can make things happen. Maybe it's getting you into an exclusive restaurant, or a special table, or backstage at a concert, or just being treated like a VIP. Friends of friends get perks, and let's face it—we all love those perks that make us feel special and look great.

Again, you don't receive because you started out by asking. You receive because you started out by giving. You offered favors and services; you made connections, expecting nothing in return. You built your network of contacts, relationships, and friends to serve others better, and what you'll wind up getting in return are life experiences that become memories that last forever.

Be Loyal

I enjoy signing some emails when appropriate as: "Your loyal friend" to people I have important relationships with.

It's not just a generic sign-off. I mean this sentiment at the deepest level. Loyalty is at the very core of who I am, so these are not just words that I type. These words have deep meaning, and I believe that the recipient feels it too.

Loyalty is critical in relationships, and I make it my job to let people know I will be there for them. Extending yourself in this way is memorable because there's a lack of loyalty in the world today. Loyalty means, "I will be there when things are out of favor for you." I won't forget you or the good things you've done for me in the past, even when you've hit a bump in the road. When someone comes upon a difficult time, being loyal to them is what makes the relationship endure.

It sucks when someone we thought of as a friend is gone because we are not of use to them anymore, or because our fortunes have turned. We can try to be careful that we aren't used or taken advantage of, but when we put ourselves out there, it's going to happen from time to time. And while we can't control other people's lack of loyalty toward us, we can be loyal when it's the other way around. When someone can no longer help us, we can still honor what they did for us in the past. We can be there for them during their tough times.

If someone's hurting, don't be afraid to reach out and talk to them. You don't need to solve their problems; you don't even need to say anything other than that you care. Sometimes when people experience a horrible turn of events, like a family crisis, a medical diagnosis, or job layoff, others do not gather around because they don't know what to say. You don't have to say anything—just reach out. The point is that you need to let them know that you are there and care about them.

Reaching out takes some courage and requires some time, but doing so forges strong, long-term relationships. Don't you always remember the ones who were there for you when you were in need? Notice I said the "ones," because it's not thousands, it's not hundreds, or maybe even ten. It's those few who show up when you're down to be there for you and who want nothing in return. I'm blessed with so many people who I can count on to always be there for me—people like Dennis Francese, who I mentioned earlier, is just one example.

John Panicali is another person I know I can count on. He is an extraordinarily gifted chiropractor and problem-solver, but he has also been one of my most loyal friends. John has truly improved my quality of life by always being there for me and never asking anything in return.

Aldona Yakobchuk is my physician's assistant, but more importantly, she's a dear and loyal friend. It's never fun to visit your physician, but thanks to Aldona, it's always a much better experience.

Another experience that can be unpleasant is air travel. And because I am fortunate enough to speak more than seventy or eighty times per year, I must fly frequently. And that's where another one of my loyal friends has made my life better. Dan D'Agostino is an expert in air traffic and has given me great advice to make my travel much smoother.

There are too many others to mention, but these relationships have changed my life for the better. I look for opportunities to help make these loyal friends' lives better, too, every chance I get. There's no preset arrangement between any of us, just each of us trying to be kinder and more caring to each other without ever wanting anything in return. Life is so much richer with these types of relationships. We must build, protect, and nourish these relationships as they are wonderful gifts. We must make sure we're always there for, and loyal to, our special friends.

Be that person who is there for others. It's a rare quality, but one that is treasured.

Be a loyal friend.

CHAPTER 14

Make a Difference in People's Lives

"It's easy to make a buck.
It's a lot tougher to make a difference."

—TOM BROKAW

Again and again, I see what a difference people can make in the lives of others. Every action we take sends ripples out into the world, as I have mentioned numerous times in this book. I know that what I do matters to others, just as I know that their actions, attention, knowledge, and kindness matter to me.

One of the biggest lessons for me of the power one person has to change the trajectory of a life came when my son, Jake, was five years old. He was playing in the driveway with the dogs when he stumbled and fell. His face hit the Belgian block stone along the driveway. And unfortunately, he landed hard.

I'll never forget the moment I got that awful phone call. I happened to be on the golf course with little concern for anything but how much break to account for on the next putt. Then it all changed. My wife couldn't even speak. Her sister, who was there, had to call me, and the first words out of her mouth were: "Jake is hurt." I didn't wait for her to finish, didn't grab my clubs, didn't even get in the golf cart. I just started running toward my car. I only lived about ten minutes away, but I probably made it there in five.

As I busted through the door, I took one look at Jake and instantly knew we had to go to the hospital *right away*.

Jake's face and clothes were full of blood. The little guy was in obvious pain, but he was really trying to be strong. We got to the hospital, and while they tended to Jake's wounds, they wanted to set up several tests because the impact occurred near his right eye. They had many concerns about a possible concussion, brain injury, or vision impairment.

We found that he had broken his nose, which would require a surgical repair. Fortunately, he did not break his orbital bone or suffer a concussion. I'll never forget how beat-up Jake looked. My little boy was exhausted by the time we finally got home. As I lay him down to sleep, his face just looked terrible, and I was very concerned about his eye. I cried as I watched him sleep. There was nothing I could do.

In time, the swelling went down, and Jake was very brave as we took him for the surgery on his nose, but we still needed to make sure his right eye was okay. The visit to the pediatric ophthalmologist revealed something that I wasn't prepared for. His right eye, the one he'd injured, turned out to be working fine and had good vision. But because we were there for an exam, the doctor also checked his left eye—not at all involved in the fall—and found some serious problems.

Jake had amblyopia in his left eye. Jake's vision in his left eye was so bad that it was causing distortion in the way he saw and interpreted images. Because of that distortion, his brain was shutting down communication to that eye. This meant that Jake was on his way to being blind in his left eye. But that communication between Jake's brain and his left eye could be improved upon if we retrained his brain before he reached the age of six. After that, it would be too late, and the communication shutdown would be irreversible.

Getting this news was awful, but at least it wasn't hopeless. We had a chance to help Jake save the vision in his eye. And if it hadn't been for the terrible accident, as bad as it was, we wouldn't have had an opportunity to try and help Jake. It's amazing how the universe works. So, in a way, I was grateful for that terrible accident.

But time was of the essence. We had less than a year to retrain Jake's brain to communicate with his bad eye. The doctor said that by putting a patch over his good eye, his brain would be forced to communicate with and look through his bad eye.

While the doctor's idea sounded like a good plan, try to keep a patch on a five-year-old kid all the time.

Jake couldn't really see much out of his bad eye to begin with, but that was all he was able to use because of the patch over his good eye. That meant the poor kid really couldn't see very well at all. To make matters worse, other kids did what kids do. Meaning, they made fun of the kid with the pirate patch. Jake, obviously, was not happy about this entire experience and was less than compliant about keeping the patch on.

We were anxious and hopeful to see if there was any improvement at the first follow-up appointment with the doctor two months after starting the patch treatment. Jake sat on my lap for the first eye test. I could see all the letters on the eye chart easily, and so could Jake...with his right eye. But when the doctor switched the machine to Jake's left eye, he could barely get past the large "E" at the top of the chart. I could clearly read the letters on the next several lines of the chart, and it broke my heart when Jake said, "I can't read anything." Jake's vision was measured at 20/200. We all know that 20/20 is normal, but Jake would have to be within 20 feet to see what someone with normal vision could see 200 feet away. The eye patch, and all of that misery, hadn't helped him to improve his vision at all.

I felt defeated. I felt I was letting my child down.

All the business successes, accolades, and accomplishments I'd achieved meant nothing. I couldn't seem to help my own son. I carried Jake out of the doctor's office. Tears rolled down my cheeks, and I couldn't make eye contact with the receptionist or those in the waiting room. And I didn't want Jake to see me cry either, because I didn't want to stress the poor boy out even more. Daddy had to be strong for him.

I knew the patch wasn't working, so I began to search for another doctor. I found a well-regarded eye physician who explained that Jake needed to be compliant for the brain to reconnect to the eye. But the doctor also understood that kids hate patches. Plus, the vision in Jake's left eye was already compromised, making it almost unbearable for him to keep the patch on. This sounded logical and made sense to me. The doctor suggested that we use a pair of glasses that would allow Jake to see better out of his left eye. But we still had to block the vision to his right eye. And so the doctor recommended we try placing duct tape over the right lens of his glasses. You read that right—freakin' duct tape—and it looked as ridiculous as it sounds. Jake hated this too.

He was just a five-year-old kid, and all he wanted to do was see. So Jake kept either taking the glasses off or peeking underneath them. If you really want to feel like a piece of shit, yell at your kid when all he's trying to do is see. But that's what I had to do—yell at Jake when he tried peeking under the glasses or taking them off.

After another two months, it was time to go back for a follow-up exam. I was hopeful as Jake sat in my lap and the chart appeared, but I was devastated when my little boy said that he couldn't see past the first two lines. My heart sank. I knew we were running out of time to save his vision.

We refused to give up and continued to search for an answer. Poetically, I learned about a highly respected eye specialist from a golf pro at the very same golf course where I had received that dreadful phone call about Jake's accident. He suggested we contact Dr. Caputo. Among Dr. Caputo's many accomplishments was an interesting story about how he had corrected pro baseball player Jay Buhner's batting stance to compensate for his poor vision in one eye, saving Buhner's baseball career. He went on to say that Dr. Caputo had an amazing reputation as an expert who can *solve problems*. It took a lot of pleading and persistence, but I was able to convince Dr. Caputo's office to allow me to bring Jake in the very next day.

From the moment I looked into Dr. Caputo's eyes and shook his hand, I could tell he was special. There are people in this world who you just know have something special about them.

He quickly glanced at Jake's duct-taped glasses and said, "That's never gonna work."

And there was something about Dr. Caputo that Jake really liked too. Did Jake pick up on his quiet confidence and optimism? I don't know. But I do know that we suddenly felt more hopeful.

Dr. Caputo examined Jake and said that he certainly needed the glasses but that the duct tape was ridiculous. There was a new treatment using the drug Atropine that Dr. Caputo was on the cutting edge of. You see, a drop of Atropine in Jake's good eye each day would dilate and blur his vision without the need for a patch or tape. No more being made fun of and no more noncompliance. Jake's brain would be forced to reconnect with his left eye. This all sounded great, but given what had happened with the past two physicians, I tempered my optimism.

Even so, time was running out. This could be our last hope.

The next two months passed quickly, and then it was time for the moment of truth—the eye exam at Dr. Caputo's office. As Jake sat in my lap, he put his small hand on my bouncing knee as if to say, "It's okay, Dad."

Jake read the first line, then the second. And then... Jake read the third and fourth lines. He couldn't go much beyond that, but we'd made progress. For the first time, we'd made progress.

We kept up with the treatment. Jake even progressed a bit further. Even so, although we are very grateful for the improvement, Jake will never have perfect vision—not even close. But at least he can use his left eye.

Jake has turned out to be a very kind and giving young man. He even dresses up like a superhero to visit terminally ill children in hospitals. Jake can do many more things because he has the use of both eyes, which have had a positive impact on Jake, but also on the lives of those he has touched. We should never underestimate the positive ripples that can occur in the lives of others from the good things we do.

I'll never be able to repay Dr. Caputo for the impact that he's had on our family's life—especially Jake's. But I can work hard every day to gain greater knowledge and expertise, just like Dr. Caputo. By always practicing this, I can be on the cutting edge in my work or be prepared so that I am able to help the clients and families that I come into contact with. That's why I push myself to continue to learn.

In my life, *I* want to be like Dr. Caputo.

I hope you do too.

CHAPTER 15

Stay Hungry

"The difference between a successful person and others is not a lack of strength, not a lack of knowledge, but rather in a lack of will."

—VINCE LOMBARDI

It's easy to be hungry when you are starved, but can you stay hungry when you are well-fed? Do you still have a desire to improve even after achieving a level of success? It's great to celebrate our wins, but it doesn't mean that our journey is over.

Staying hungry in business can help you grow and stay ahead of your competition. But it's also important to stay hungry in your personal relationships. Are you nurturing the relationships that are already established, or are some of them taken for granted?

One of the biggest reasons why relationships turn sour is that people can feel unappreciated. Clients, employees, and lovers will all stick by your side longer if they feel that you appreciate them. Remember the little things you did when you wanted to gain someone's favor? If we continue to treat those relationships in a way that makes them feel special and appreciated, we will not only see those relationships endure; we will see them continue to reach higher levels.

Sometimes knowing how we can improve ourselves and our relationships is obvious. It can be as easy as looking back and repeating the little things that led us to success, like staying hungry for improvement. But sometimes we don't know how we can take ourselves to the next level or how we can fix and improve a relationship that is struggling.

Oftentimes, it's difficult to see the path toward improvement because we're in the middle of it all. It's hard to gain perspective when you're at the center of the problem. When we're in this situation, this is where we can use some help or coaching.

First, ask yourself if you are coachable. It's important to be honest because it's not easy to be coachable. It's hard to let go of control and admit that someone else may know more than you do about your own situation. Being coachable takes an open mind, a deep desire to improve, and a large amount of humility. If you don't feel that you are very coachable, then you must work toward this goal. Even the most successful people in business, sports, and life have reaped the benefits of being coached. Being coachable allows you to gain perspective and take advantage of experiences that others have had and that you don't have to pay the price of going through.

But while you may gain a lot from a good coaching experience, that doesn't mean you must blindly take every bit of advice and adhere to it. It's okay to make small adjustments so that the coaching best fits you. It's also paramount that you find a coach who you can trust.

I once had the pleasure of sharing the stage with Dallas Cowboys coaching legend Tom Landry. I loved his perspective on staying hungry. I remember him saying, "I see these players today who celebrate like crazy when they score a touchdown." He went on, "It's okay to celebrate, but when a player goes hog-wild and over-celebrates one touchdown, I'm really not afraid of that guy." He paused. "That guy celebrating like he won the lottery for just one score must feel like it's a surprise. Like he got lucky. Like it was not supposed to happen. That's why I'm not afraid of him. But you know who I am afraid of? I'm afraid of the guy who scored a touchdown on us and did it like he was just doing his job. Like he was *supposed* to score on you. It's where he belongs, and he makes you feel like he's gonna do it again. *That's* the guy I'm afraid of."

Great lesson here. Yes, celebrate and have fun, *but you shouldn't be shocked by winning; you should expect to win.*

I see this in business all the time. People have a great month or a great year and then take their foot off the gas. They reach a certain level of success, but then they don't keep striving. It's almost like it becomes beneath them to continue to put in the hard work at their new level of success. They read a book or hear that they should work less and take more time off. Yes, I get it; you shouldn't be "all work" twenty-four-seven, but so many people use this mentality as an excuse to slow down, which hurts their growth.

Each success isn't an end. It's just another step, another milestone.

I enjoy and recognize my wins, but I don't throw a party every time I close a deal. When I break through to a new level or reach a goal ahead of schedule, I don't slow down; I set a new, higher goal to reach.

Successful people who can stay hungry, even when they're well-fed, understand that the big wins are expected. For them, the big wins are milestones, not destinations. That's critical if you want to be a winner in the long term. You seldom can live off one win, and the joy of making winning a habit is much more fulfilling.

It's also a lot easier for us to stay hungry when we can understand what motivates us most.

So Get in Touch with <u>Your</u> "Why"

Why do you go to work each day? Think about it. When you walk out the door of your home, are you thinking about the reasons you are doing so, or are you just getting in the car and turning on the radio? Are you just going through your routine, or are you moving with a purpose in mind? Guess which will bring you better results.

There must be a reason, a goal, or a motivation to do what you do; otherwise, it becomes a much more difficult grind. We must understand the "why" behind the work we are doing, and that "why" can come in many forms.

Is it money? We know that money doesn't buy everything, but it sure does help. There is no shame in having financial goals or desires. If using money as a motivator can help you to better achieve your objectives at work, then you need to keep that in mind. You can do a lot of good for others if you have additional dollars to do it with.

Competition can also be an effective motivator. We all have some measure of a competitive spirit in us, and we want to be the best. Use your competitive energy to work harder, stay later, make another call, practice or learn so you can improve, and do whatever it takes to win or beat your previous goals. When you successfully achieve a goal, set the bar higher.

We know how important self-confidence is. Besting your previous high mark will go a long way toward improving it. Can you beat your best sales year or month, week or day? I always look to do better than my previous highest level, and not just in sales. I want my relationships and interactions to be better today than they have ever been. I want the speaking presentation I am giving today to be the best one I have ever given. Whatever it is, I want the current one to be the best I have done yet.

If you ask me, "What was the best _____ I have ever done?" I want the answer to be, "My most recent one, but I think my next one will be even better!"

There is something very powerful in knowing that you are at your all-time best...right now! No looking back, no going back, no longing for the good old days. Think about how your self-confidence will soar when you know that you are the very best version of yourself right now. Make this a part of your "why."

Your significant other is likely a very big part of your life. If you truly want to make a better life for that person, remember that when you walk out the door in the morning. Perhaps wanting to hear your significant other sincerely say that they are proud of you could be just the motivation you need to reach higher.

Our parents, so often, make countless sacrifices to provide us with opportunity. The desire to honor the sacrifices my parents have made has been very motivational for me. I want to make sure I'm not wasting my abilities, talents, and opportunities provided to me.

Would you walk through fire for your children? Chances are, you would. In fact, we probably would do just about anything for our children. Keeping that in mind every day is powerful and will help you get through challenges at work—and not just "get through" them. It will also make you want to accomplish greater goals so that you can give your children the best life possible and do more for your kids than was done for you.

It's amazing to me that all the important points just listed are often far from the thoughts that go through our minds every day at work. Imagine what can be achieved if we were to keep our "why" at the forefront of our minds when we walk out the door each morning in pursuit of our careers. Success is almost inevitable because there is no way we'd let our children down, disappoint our parents, shortchange our significant other or, most importantly, cheat ourselves out of the bigger and better things in life that we didn't think were attainable. Don't think you don't deserve those things. Don't think small. You need to think and dream big.

Think Bigger

Thinking big sounds like it should be easy to do. But it's not that easy, because thinking big is a skill we need to learn, practice, and refine every day.

Most of us don't think big; doing so seldom crosses our minds. If it does, we often quickly dismiss our ideas as being too crazy or beyond our reach.

Being so poor growing up, I was thrilled to just taste success. I had dreams, and they were big, but I didn't know how to make them come true. All that changed in my mid-twenties when I met Jack Grumet.

Jack, a true entrepreneur, had a wonderful ability to take ideas to a large scale—talk about staying hungry! If a normal, or even gifted, entrepreneur started a small restaurant, their primary focus would be on making a profit. But Jack would focus on making a franchise! He did this time and again in shopping malls, in the securities industry, and by creating a company that he eventually took public—Manhattan Bagel. I was fortunate to be introduced to Jack, but even more fortunate that he took a liking to me.

Jack became a mentor. He took an interest in my business and offered advice. He didn't have the detailed knowledge of my day-to-day operations, but he had something more valuable: vision. He taught me how to think of my business on a much bigger level. My eyes were opened. I expanded my mortgage business, as well as every business or endeavor after that. From being featured in a local paper to being seen on local TV; from appearing on local TV to appearing on national TV; from speaking in a small office to speaking to entire industries; from a small musical to a global brand in *Rock of Ages*, my business career changed forever.

When you change your perspective, when you take a much bigger view and move in that direction, you will be amazed at what will happen for you.

There have been, and still are, many mentors in my life—and I am sure I will have other mentors. I have also been a mentor to many. I have helped launch the speaking careers of several talented individuals. I have also mentored founders of very successful businesses that have been sold for millions of dollars. By being a mentor, I learned something very important: successful people like creating protégés. That means that you can find people who will *want* to help you...*for free*. You just need to get them to like you. You do this by putting in the hard work in advance, making progress in your business, and learning and gaining expertise. Then find a potential mentor and show them the respect of learning about them before you meet.

Mentors are often naturally curious and hungry to learn about other businesses, and you can tell them about yours. Don't be surprised if they offer valuable insights and suggestions. Follow up on their ideas and let them know how you did. Before you know it, you have a mentor.

I Wanna Rock

If you've ever met someone who speaks several languages, you may think of that individual as very intelligent. But when someone has success in a particular type of business, the outside world wants to pigeon-hole them solely into that business, as if it was their only area of expertise. That's far from the truth. Just as people who learn one language often find learning a second or a third easier, strategies you learn in one field of business can be applied in another with great results, even though the industries may be totally different and present different challenges.

Having started and grown several businesses in different industries, I've learned not to be fearful of starting new business ventures that are unrelated to my previous businesses. I did this when I went from selling stereos to real estate to mortgages. Or when I went from writing articles for local newspapers to TV to speaking to writing this book. I also did this when I entered into subscription-based financial businesses like Mortgage Market Guide, MBS Highway, and Social Survey. I even crossed over to a successful high-end medical imaging practice, which I built and then sold. I remained hungry but not just in my primary business; I was hungry for knowledge, challenges, and successes in new ventures.

It's only natural to hesitate or to be fearful of entering into a new venture, especially if it's in a completely different vertical from where you're most comfortable. But you need to remember that, just like learning a new language, you can learn a new business if you surround yourself with a great team.

There's something very exciting about entering a new arena. One of those thrilling arenas for me was entertainment. I had lots of experience on stage as well as on camera, so when I had the opportunity to act in a Hollywood film, I didn't hesitate to go for it! Acting is less glamorous than I first thought, though. It's also much more difficult than just being myself on stage or TV because taking on a different persona is hard. It made acting a big challenge for me and gave me a new perspective on how talented other actors are. Even though I worked hard to be coachable and was doing everything my coach (the director) said to do, it was still quite difficult, and I sucked at times. But with hard work and lots of effort, I did okay.

I enjoyed my acting experience, which grew to include speaking roles in several films and even making the trailer for a movie called *Barry Munday*. (It's a very funny and heartwarming movie with a terrific cast. You should check it out if you haven't done so already—at least the trailer, which cracked up my editor!). But the best thing that came out of the film experience was being introduced to the script for the theatrical production of *Rock of Ages*. I fell in love with the story and the music from the very beginning and put up most of the money to bring the show to Broadway.

Rock of Ages is the twenty-seventh longest-running show in Broadway history. It's critically acclaimed. The show has toured the U.S. and the world, playing in London, Australia, Toronto, Las Vegas, and many parts of Asia. It was even made into a major motion picture starring Tom Cruise. I got to play the record producer in the movie. *Rock of Ages* is a financially successful endeavor that has allowed me to develop some incredible relationships, friendships, and introductions to many A-list players in sports and entertainment. They love coming to the show and will even contact me directly on my cell phone to attend.

An important component in the success of any business is the team behind it. And this was no different with *Rock of Ages*, where I tried to assemble the best team I could. Randi Zuckerberg, who invented Facebook Live and is a well-known social media visionary as well as a successful author, always provides valuable input. As Randi mentioned in the foreword, she played the role of Regina (pronounced rah-JIE-nuh) in *Rock of Ages* and has an amazing singing voice.

Future Baseball Hall-of-Famer, Carlos Beltran, also asked to become a partner with his wife, Jessica. He has been helpful in arranging events like "Yankee Night" at the show, which has been instrumental in garnering nationwide media coverage.

Tony Robbins is a partner who has helped to spread awareness about the show. Other notable partners include Peter Boockvar, Kenny Dichter, Ed Moldaver, Kevin Peranio, Eddy Perez, and my long-time entertainment partner, Scott Prisand.

Having these incredible leaders and friends as partners in the show helped enable the success of this project. *Rock of Ages* was nominated for five Tony Awards, including Best Musical. Building a team that adds value through knowledge and influence will greatly increase your odds of winning.

Plus, Randi Zuckerberg isn't the only one who likes to sing and perform. A few years back, I started a band inspired by *Rock of Ages*. It began as a tiny little group playing for free just to get noticed. I knew we were good, but we needed more exposure. So I asked some well-known singers who had appeared in the Broadway musical do some gigs with us. This strategy goes back to the idea of "thinking big." We went from playing bars with fifty people to performing in front of a couple thousand people. It doesn't matter if it's a business or a band, thinking big will transform your experience. Playing on a bigger scale happened because I wanted it, reached for it, and asked for it.

It's wonderful how your life changes when you think bigger and stay hungry.

CHAPTER 16

Be a Teacher

"Give a man a fish, and you feed him for a day. Teach a man to fish, and you feed him for a lifetime."

—ANCIENT PROVERB

The best way to learn is often by teaching. Most people aren't aware of this or don't think it sounds logical. They feel you have to be an expert before you start teaching someone else. But the truth is that you gain expertise when you teach.

As you begin teaching, you start thinking more deeply about how to tie together all the parts of the concept that you're talking about. You must logically articulate the concept from start to finish so that you can explain it to someone else—especially if they start asking you questions. You find the holes and then do the research to fill them. Do not underestimate the power of teaching. We all have learned things that we may have either forgotten or that are a little foggy in our brains. When we teach these concepts, it forces us to refresh and store the ideas in our minds.

Teaching is a highly effective way to expand our knowledge and expertise. Lacking the confidence to teach others just because you don't know the whole story yet will rob you of an accelerated learning experience.

Now, I'm not suggesting that you start giving golf lessons if you've never picked up a club in your life. But you don't have to be a golf pro to assist a beginner if you have some experience playing. By assisting them, you can reinforce your own fundamentals.

Empower Instead of Rescue

Don't just rescue somebody. That does them a disservice. They miss the opportunity to learn what they need to do for themselves.

As an advisor, I want to empower the people I meet so they can take control of their lives and money. This means not just giving them the answer but also taking them along the journey of *how* I arrived at the answer. By teaching them the path, they can find the way.

At MBS Highway, I help over 20,000 mortgage professionals decide whether they should advise their customers to lock or float their mortgage rate. I don't ever just give advice without explaining the rationale for how I came to my conclusion. I also record a video each morning that my subscribers watch and learn from. Over the years, this has resulted in elevating the entire mortgage industry's knowledge of financial markets, as well as helped to transform mortgage salespeople into advisors. Because of this responsibility, I am committed to continuously learning and staying sharp. I always have to find valuable insights to share. Teaching makes me better.

Avoid "Should"

As a teacher or advisor, the verbiage you use with your students or clients is important. For example, "should" can be a dirty word in advising. It's a trigger word that can make the listener feel as if they're already failing. Saying "You should be saving more for retirement" can be a bit insulting. Try rephrasing it as, "Many people find that saving just an extra $100 per week for retirement can result in tens of thousands of dollars in additional retirement savings." Or try to frame your suggestions and advice as options, then back them up with information about why a choice has beneficial results. It's not easy to avoid "should," but you "should" try.... Just kidding.

Use Stories and Examples

People love stories. So fill your lessons with stories and examples to give context and bring those lessons to life, just like I've tried to do with you throughout this book.

Always try to give credit where credit is due. For example, try saying, "I've learned this from _____, and here's how I've applied it and how it has benefited me."

Finding Their Why

We've talked about finding *your* "why," but your clients are motivated by *their* "why." The best way to find *their* "why" is by asking questions...and asking them more than once and in different ways. Your client's first answer might be what they *think* they want you to hear, but digging deeper often helps you get to the root of what's really important to them. That's where you can make a better connection with your client. Chances are, they don't realize that structuring

MONEY IN THE STREETS

the transaction differently may help bring them closer to one of their goals. Just like you, they need to get in touch with what motivates them. Maybe it's their kids, or money, or their significant other.

People often start at "price" or "cost," but value comes from helping people receive what they really need. Remember, the real value that your clients need most can be different from what they think they want. It's up to you to discover what's most important by finding their "why."

Let me tell you a quick story. I love to travel and have been fortunate enough to visit Pompeii, Italy, twice. History fascinates me, and I can't help but think about what it would have been like to go back in time to see how people lived. That's why I love Pompeii. Back in 79 A.D., Mt. Vesuvius erupted, and Pompeii was quickly covered in ash. Because this was ash and not lava, and because it happened so fast, Pompeii was preserved just as it was 2,000 years ago. Over the past century, two-thirds of the city has been uncovered, so we can see just how people lived back then. As you walk through the streets, it is mind-blowing to observe that these people had ways of dealing with all of the same challenges and needs that we have today.

We can tell that they liked being entertained, gathering, and shopping. They even liked fast food—along the main thoroughfares, you can see that there were businesses designed to provide cooked food for Pompeiians on the go. I remember pointing to one such storefront and saying,

"This must've been like their version of McDonald's." I sure gained a tremendous amount of historical knowledge from my visit, but here's my big takeaway: people have the same basic needs or desires.

It doesn't matter where they're from or what time period they lived in. People are similar, and they often want the same things. They have goals they want to reach and fears to overcome. They want to feel important; they want to feel special; they want to feel loved.

Don't overcomplicate your business and your relationships. Chances are if you feel it, they feel it too.

CHAPTER 17

Work With Fear

"I learned that courage was not the absence of fear, but the triumph over it. The brave man is not he who does not feel afraid, but he who conquers that fear."

—NELSON MANDELA

Fear can be debilitating; it can also be motivating. Fear is a big influencer...and the media knows this well.

Fear is a powerful force in all of our lives. And this is no accident. As humans, our most basic need is survival. Fear exists to alert us to danger and keep us alive.

The survival part of our brain is the amygdala, which causes time to slow down when we are fearful. This happens so we can remember times of danger to learn how to avoid the negative outcome from reoccurring in the future. These moments actually imprint on your brain. Remember where you were when you got the horrible news about 9/11? We all do. It's imprinted. And we all have so many of these scary incidents etched in our minds. I'm sure you can recall hearing some bad news about a loved one or a frightening event that happened to you. Maybe it was even saying that first "I love you" to someone. Yeah, that's a different kind of scary, but it was still scary. All those reactions to fear are your amygdala at work. By making sure to slow time down, you can remember even the tiny details, like where you were or the time on the clock. This helps you stay alert to and recognize a dangerous pattern, which keeps you safe for the next time. It's a miraculous survival tool, but it's a really lousy one when it comes to relationships and business.

I mentioned that the media knows all too well how the amygdala works. Since I have been on TV for many years, I've seen firsthand how things get twisted and sensationalized to scare you. "It's the storm of the century," or "The market will crash," or "Buy a mask so you don't die from bird flu or swine flu," or whatever will grab your attention. Yikes! We know these events almost never match the media hype. Then why does the media evoke fear? Because they know you will likely tune in, pay attention, and remember it. That increases their viewership ratings and allows them to charge more for advertising.

Savvy marketers know how the amygdala works too. They want you to remember their message, so they play on the Fear of Missing Out, a.k.a. FOMO.

If we are aware of how our brain tries to protect us with this system, we can often overcome the many negative aspects of this survival mechanism. Fear of a bad outcome can cause us to enter a state of denial. We may talk ourselves into believing a lie because it feels nicer and easier than having to face the truth or the changes that it might bring.

Anxiety is another terribly stressful result that fear can bring. We want certainty, but there are many things we can't control. We become consumed with the "what ifs" and have a very hard time focusing. This is not an easy spiral to get out of, which is why we need to assess the fear.

Having an alarm system of any kind can be critical to maintaining our safety, but we all know that false alarms are a negative side effect of having that alarm system.

If you leave popcorn in the microwave a bit too long and it starts to smoke, the smoke alarm will go off with a piercing sound. Okay, so you may have to put the popcorn bag in the sink before throwing it out, fan the smoke so it clears, and maybe do a bit of cleanup...but you know everything is going to be okay. You don't run out of the house yelling and screaming after spraying your fire extinguisher all over your kitchen and dialing 911 just because the smoke alarm went off.

You understand that the alarm is there to help you, but at this point, the alarm noise is just annoying because there is no real danger. You correctly override the smoke alarm system because you understand what is happening. We must train ourselves to assess our internal fear alarm system the same way. Yeah, your amygdala is going to kick in hard, hindering your ability to focus and move forward, but are you being held back because you are *feeling* afraid, or is there actual danger? Fear can throw off our ability to reason and understand that the situation may not really be terrible or dangerous.

Think about it—so what if the client says no, or your idea isn't the hit you thought it would be? Or even if the object of your affection doesn't say "I love you" back? Is the undesired response really *that* devastating or dangerous? Your amygdala can't tell the difference—it is either alerting you, or it's not. That's why *you* have to assess the fear you are feeling.

It's interesting how many people avoid or postpone making calls that can be a bit uncomfortable. This can be detrimental to our business, but it is also problematic in relationships. We often fear reaching out to someone who is going through a tough time—but that's just the thing that makes the relationship deeper and more enduring. We can be fearful of reaching out to get help or advice because we don't want to show weakness—but the other person may be appreciative that you are seeking their council. And their help could be just what you need to move ahead. Don't let fear stop you.

Whatever the circumstances, take a breath and ask yourself, *what is the worst that can* happen? How tough is the recovery if it doesn't work out? What will I lose? And most importantly, *how bad will I feel because I chickened out*?

Some kids are a bit scared of amusement park rides, and it holds them back from having fun. They often later discover that it's much worse to sit on the sidelines and watch others experience joys that they are missing out on. I can sure relate to that, and maybe you can too. It sucked to not go on the ride. But once I pushed through, I was both happy and proud.

I mentioned my crazy childhood friends, David Augenblick and Craig Frankel. These guys made every day exciting. They were fun-loving but had a mischievous side... especially David, who had a way of bringing out the mischievous side in me as well. There are far too many stories to talk about that exemplify just how crazy it was to grow up with these guys. But I will share one that will help clarify why working with fear is so important.

Back in my early twenties, David, Craig, and I brought three dates on a camping trip. We were always of a curious mindset and loved to explore. As we hiked through the woods, we came upon a cliff overlooking a beautiful secluded lake that was about fifty feet below us. Never in my wildest dreams would I have had even the slightest thought of jumping off this cliff into the lake. And for that matter, I didn't think any other normal human would have that type of thought. But I was with David and Craig, and as they both started discussing what it might be like to jump off, I still felt safe that there was no chance that anyone would actually go through with this. But again, I was with David and Craig.

We also had our hot dates, who now became interested in seeing if any of us would actually take the plunge. I should also mention that I've always been a bit uncomfortable with heights, so while the others had no problem going to the edge of the cliff to look down, I gingerly approached the edge but kept a safe few feet away from the tip. Honestly, I would have been hesitant even if there had been a guard-rail. But, of course, there was no guardrail; there was no smooth platform, just uneven rocks and a fifty-foot drop.

I suggested that, while the view was great, we should now be making our way along the hike. But David had become intrigued with making the jump. By this time, he had garnered a cheering section from the girls, who were egging him on. Before the words could come out of my mouth that it would be too crazy for him to do this, David had positioned himself to get a running start. I looked on in disbelief as he flung his body off the cliff and jumped into the lake below.

David surfaced, screaming about how awesome it was, and how Craig and I *had to do this!* "Come on, it's great!" Of course, the girls were cheering for David too. I wanted no part of it and locked eyes with Craig with a look that said *you're not really thinking about doing this, right?* But I could tell that, with the girls now cheering Craig on, he had made up his mind to follow David in. I was speechless, and Craig was airborne. The next thing I knew, the two of them were yelling and hugging and high-fiving in the water. The girls, who were now standing next to me, cheering for the guys, all turned their heads in my direction with a look that said...*well?*

I was terrified to make the jump, but I also didn't want to be viewed as a wimp. I thought, *who could blame me for not doing something so crazy? I'm actually the smart one here.* But the hollers from below were echoing, "Barry, Barry, come on! Come on! You're gonna love it!" I had a choice to make, but really, there was no choice. I looked at my date and knew at that very moment that I *had* to do this.

As mentioned, I'm not great with heights, and I didn't want to take a chance on tripping over the uneven rocks. So I didn't do the bold running start like David and Craig. Instead, I very timidly went over the edge, and that's when I almost shit myself.

You see, because I had not looked down prior to jumping, I didn't realize that there were rocks right under the cliff. So I had to wiggle my body just enough to clear them. Since I was floundering and flopping around as I hit the water, it created quite a smack in some sensitive spots. Not the most glamorous entry in front of the three girls watching from above, but I didn't care about that at the time. I sank a lot deeper than I thought I would but never touched the bottom. It felt like it took forever to surface, and as I was coming up to get air, I couldn't help but think, *Why didn't those fuckers tell me how bad this would hurt? They left that part out!*

When I surfaced, the boys hugged and high-fived me. And I felt incredible. The girls cheered for me, and the exhilarating feeling stayed with me for a long time. *I had overcome my fear.*

I had a choice to make that day: either give in to my fear or get past it. As I write this story and share this memory with you, that wonderful feeling comes back to me, causes a tingle in my body, and puts a smile on my face. Here's the thing: I am certain that if I hadn't taken that jump, I would have regretted it then and still have regretted it to this very day. I've never taken a jump off a cliff like that again—nor do I feel the need to. I'm satisfied knowing I've done it once.

Fear is real, and sometimes, you should hold back. But I bet you that when you take an honest look back at the times in your life when you were faced with fear, you likely have much less regret about risks you took to gain experiences and far more regrets about the experiences that you let fear take from you.

CHAPTER 18

Bad Things Happen, But We Can Still Control Our Mindset

"We must be willing to let go of the life we've planned, so as to have the life that is waiting for us."

—JOSEPH CAMPBELL

In 2012, on a speaking trip to Columbus, Ohio, I got together with some friends who took me to a local restaurant known for delicious and very spicy fried chicken. It wasn't the healthiest meal in the world, but man, it was tasty! It was so spicy that I can remember literally sweating at the table. It seemed like the only way to cool the fire in my mouth was to take yet *another* bite and postpone the agony.

As to be expected, the excessive spice, along with the greasy meal, caught up with me that evening. I was chomping on Tums like they were potato chips in an attempt to reduce the flame in my esophagus. Many of us have had heartburn before, but this night was different.

The antacids helped, but they didn't put out the fire. Even more worrisome, the heartburn persisted for a few days.

I couldn't ignore it.

My hectic speaking schedule had me getting ready for my next trip to San Francisco, but the heartburn was still there—and it had been almost a week since it began.

Luckily, right across the hall from my office was a gastroenterology practice. I knew one of the physicians, Dr. Gold, who had become a friend as we often ran into each other in the parking lot and stopped to chat.

I called him on his cell phone and explained what was going on. I said, "I'm leaving for San Francisco tomorrow afternoon. Any chance you can prescribe something for me before I hop on the plane?" The doctor explained that he wouldn't be in for the next couple of days, but he scheduled me to see another physician. That's when I met Dr. Barbara Cencora. She did an exam, and afterwards, she handed me some samples of Omeprazole that would likely help on the condition that I set up an endoscopy for after my trip to make sure everything was okay. I agreed; the pain was so bad I would've agreed to just about anything.

So off I went to California—pills in hand—and sure enough, they worked like magic. Two days later, I had forgotten all about the pain I'd been in. When I returned from California, I asked my assistant to call Dr. Cencora's office to cancel the endoscopy.... I was fine now and really busy. I didn't need a stupid test.

My assistant called the doctor's office to cancel the scan, but then I heard her say, "Barry, the doctor wants to talk to you." I picked up the phone and did my best to charm my way out of the endoscopy, but Dr. Cencora was tough. She *made* me agree to go through with the appointment and give my word. Now I was obligated. You see, if it were my buddy, Dr. Gold, I could've easily talked my way out of the endoscopy. But the universe had different plans for me and wanted me to have this test done.

A couple of weeks later, I went for the endoscopy, and it wasn't so bad. While in recovery, and still a bit groggy, Dr. Cencora said, "Everything looks good, but I saw a little tiny something that I'm sure is nothing." She continued, "But

I want to be completely certain, so I sent it to pathology." Quite honestly, I was more concerned about returning the dozens of emails and texts I had seen on my phone than her comments about some remote concern that was probably nothing to worry about anyway.

A couple of weeks later, I was alone in my office after hours wrapping up. It was August 20, 2012, at 5:35 p.m. My phone rang, and it was Dr. Cencora. The call started out fine, until she said, "We got the report back from pathology, and you have non-Hodgkin's follicular lymphoma."

I really didn't understand what that meant, and more importantly, what it meant for me....

I think I asked her three different times and in three different ways to explain further. It didn't really sink in until she said, "Barry, you have cancer."

It's funny how your senses react when you hear something shocking. I couldn't really hear the rest of what she was saying, and it didn't make much sense; I was still in denial. Everything slowed down. I can still remember everything about where I was, even the time on the clock. I had to do my best to gather myself because I now had so many questions. *How was this going to affect me? Will this impact my longevity? Are there any changes I need to make?* Essentially, *what happens next?*

I stood up at my desk, stared out the window, and then looked at a picture on my desk of me and my youngest son, Jared. *What would I say? How would I break the news to my family?* *What am I going to tell Jared?* These questions went through my head as I looked at his face in the picture.

As I tried to gather myself, to find any bit of hope or encouragement I could, Dr. Cencora went on to say, "We were really lucky to catch this in its very early stages."

I quickly thought of all the things that had to happen for this discovery to be made: the trip to Ohio, the spicy chicken, Dr. Cencora being tough and forcing me to do the test...and, most importantly, trusting her gut to be extra cautious and send a sample biopsy. It was bad news, but I was lucky for the series of events that allowed this to be found early.

The "C-word" was my new reality.

Luckily, in the words of my doctor, the diagnosis "should not affect your longevity." That was a positive, but I still had to figure out how I was going to tell my family. That night, I only discussed it with my wife. Like me, she was in denial at first. I reassured her that this was going to turn out okay as tears ran down her face. She didn't say much as she grabbed my hand and held it for a while. We knew we had work to do.

I clung to the message that it had been detected early and should not affect my longevity. It was bad news, but I remained optimistic and grateful because it could have been much worse.

I decided not to tell my children right away. I lacked information and needed to do my research before I spoke with them. I knew that researching my condition on the internet was probably not the best approach, but I couldn't help myself. The more I read, the more nervous I became. Fortunately, I had built up contacts, relationships, and friends who could help or could point me to others who could help.

I spent the next days and weeks learning. I read everything I could get my hands on and talked to any doctor I knew or friend I had. I saw oncologists and endocrinologists.

I needed to understand everything I could about what was inside me. But first, I needed to understand why.

I learned that my cancer was caused by a bacterial infection called H. pylori that can be contracted through food. So, considering all the travel and eating out I'd done on the road, I was at a higher risk for contracting it. H. pylori is not contagious and can lurk in your gut without symptoms like it did for me. I didn't know I was carrying that bacteria in my body. Once I found out, a simple course of antibiotics cured me of the bacteria. Such an easy fix—if you know you have it. Unfortunately, I didn't know for a long time because there were no symptoms. It can be dangerous to have H. pylori go untreated because one out of every 200 people who carry the H. pylori bacteria for an extended period of time eventually develop this type of cancer.

I had won the worst lottery.

On the bright side (I'm always looking for a bright side), the recommended treatment for me was to do nothing.

There is no course of action to take for this type of cancer, unless it becomes aggressive, except to be monitored every six months through scans and bloodwork. And, for even more good news, if and when this cancer becomes aggressive, it can be responsive to treatment with Rituxan. This is less traumatic than chemotherapy. Either way, in my mind, I was running with this prognosis as a good thing. I *was* lucky. And I'm going to use this to take an even more grateful perspective and have a higher level of appreciation for what I would normally take for granted.

I don't ever pity myself, and I typically don't even talk about the cancer. This book is the first time that I have been public about it...more than seven years later. Many people who know me will be surprised to learn about the illness. I don't feel I'm a victim. I don't want people to feel sorry for me. And I certainly don't want to use this in any way to gain an advantage by being that "poor me" guy who you should take it easy on.

I still have to get scans and bloodwork done every six months when I go to visit my oncologist, Dr. Balar, who has become a friend. Have I mentioned that I'm a baby when it comes to having my blood drawn? One of Dr. Balar's many phlebotomists, Sam, is my girl for drawing blood. Everyone there knows she is the only one I let do it. Sam even uses the baby needle for me. Each visit is always friendly and cordial, but I'm also always holding my breath and become very serious as I wait for the results of the bloodwork. It's spun right there, so you know the results very quickly, and my heart always races until I hear Dr. Balar say, "We're good." It's the same with the endoscopy scans, which Dr. Cencora performs for me. Each time, I had been fortunate to hear her say, "No change, Barry. Go back to your life."

But the very last scan, there *was* a change. As I was recovering, Dr. Cencora said for the first time, "Barry, I didn't even see anything this time." I said, "Say that again, doc. I want to make sure I'm not dreaming." She said, "Really, it looks better. I mean it. I don't see anything, but I still have to send the sample to pathology."

Could a miracle just have happened? I was so fucking happy; I think I hugged and kissed six or seven of the ladies working there! And I definitely high-fived some guy getting ready to go in for his colonoscopy.

About a week later, Dr. Cencora called. I was expecting the news to set off a celebration and opening of some really expensive wine. I could hear it in my mind...how would she tell me? What would the words be? *You're clear, Barry. It's all good. No more cancer.*

But that wasn't what she said. She said, "It's still there. For some reason, it seems to have quieted down, but it's there. We'll just keep doing what we've been doing, and if things change, we'll address it."

So many thoughts ran through my mind. Of course, I was very disappointed...but nothing had really changed. I was still okay. The cancer is still there—another random event. I can't control the cancer, so all I can do is try to change my mindset.

Change your focus. Change your mindset. And you can change the world.

By focusing on all the wonderful people and things I have in my life, I am spending less time in a state of worry. I admit that when the tests are conducted, I do think about how my life would change if I received bad news, which causes me to feel anxious. But I still keep a very positive outlook. I want to do a lot more in my life, and I want to be a positive influence on others. Not just on my children and family members, but on anyone who is experiencing a time of difficulty or wanting more in their life. If I am over-whelmed with negative thoughts and worry, I will be unable to make the most of what I have.

Each of us has troubles. They don't have to be health-re-lated. Maybe it's work, or family, or a love relationship. It's hard to stop thinking about these problems when they are acute and serious. However, it helps to understand the differences between those circumstances that are in our control and those that are not.

If there really is something that we can do to help a bad situation, we should spend much of our time and energy focusing on a possible solution. But when we are faced with a bad situation, one that we have no control over—like I am with my cancer—all the focus, time, energy, and worry feeds into the negativity and just makes it worse. We may even become paralyzed and unable to do anything else.

It's in these times that we must change focus. We must distract ourselves from the uncontrollable problem and find something to pour our energy into. This could be family, a project you are passionate about, a cause, or maybe your business or line of work. Perhaps you can help educate others on how to avoid or deal with their problems, as I have tried to do in this book. Rather than being stuck in worry, find opportunities to do the most good with your time and energy.

Grab opportunities because they are all around you...

Just like the money in the streets.

AFTERWORD

When I was first asked to write the afterword for Barry's book, the only thought that ran through my head was, *Oh shit! Oh shit!* I wish I could share something more profound with you, but it's true.

I've been a huge fan of Barry's for a while, and now, I am fortunate enough to call him my friend. I'm an executive in the mortgage industry, and naturally, I learned of Barry then, since he influences what the rates are doing, what we need to bring to the market to make it nice and healthy, and how we should be advising our mortgage professionals.

One quality has always struck me about him.

He is kind.

If you spend any amount of time listening to him, his intentions become very clear. No matter who he is speaking to, whether he is being interviewed on a podcast or appearing on Fox News—where he is a regular—the caring way he treats others accompanies everything he does.

Barry has become not just a person I look up to; he is a person I learn from. He is a person who brings value and meaning to the lives of everyone he touches. I listen to Barry frequently, and on occasion, he says, "I want to be like so-and-so." It's my turn today to tell Barry, I wish more people not only wanted to be more like you but that they *were* more like you.

The world could use more kindness right about now. I am as positive as they come, but I know that you can never go wrong when you are kind.

That is the theme of Barry's book. It's not just the story of how he bootstrapped his way to become a multipreneur who sets the bar for the rest of us. It's the story of how Barry never forgot who he was as he told his story to help other people. It's the way he stays in the moment to look a person in the eye and let them know he cares about what they are going to say. It's how he hugs the attendant at a ball game and expresses how much he cares about them and their day.

The memories of how he grew up aren't far from Barry's mind, and you'll read that for yourself in this book. He doesn't have any regrets about growing up in such a hard-scrabble existence. And where other people might try to forget difficult circumstances like his, I swear he wants to remember them. He wants to never lose touch with that little boy. I wasn't surprised to read that, even as a kid, Barry wanted more and knew he would have it one day.

Afterword

Isn't that the mark of every great leader?

I don't think Barry has any idea of how, by simply living his life, he has become such an inspiration to so many. Just by getting up and doing what he does, he moves people to be better and expect more of themselves. And don't get me wrong, Barry is one of the top producers; he always has been. But Barry also wants people to stay grounded as they rise up through the ranks as he has. He wants to combine grinding away in the office with considering the right choices and reexamining what is best for the team, "even if we've always done it this way."

From Coach Bill Belichick, who offers memorable coaching advice that you can use in the boardroom, to the lessons he learned as a Broadway producer and the innovation he demonstrated even when he sold stereos out of the trunk of his car, the stories of *Money in the Streets* will remain with you long after you've read the last page.

That's his style. He has to make a splash in this world for the better, and that's exactly what he's done with his first book.

Enjoy it.

Then read it again and again to improve your business and every relationship in your life.

I love you, brother.

—*Jonny Fowler*, Best-selling author of *Here's Jonny: Tales of Gratitude from the Oilfield to the Boardroom*

ABOUT THE AUTHOR

Barry Habib is a successful American entrepreneur and founder of multiple enterprising businesses. A frequent media authority with a long tenure and monthly appearances on CNBC and FOX, he is sought after for his mortgage and housing expertise.

As the CEO of MBS Highway, Barry developed the platform that helps mortgage professionals better understand the interest rate environment and helps real estate agents articulate client opportunities. To date, MBS Highway is the industry's most highly regarded tool for transforming salespeople into advisors.

In 2017 and 2019, Barry was named Zillow and Pulsenomics's top Real Estate Forecaster and was presented with the Crystal Ball Award for the most accurate real estate forecasts surpassing the 150 top economists in the US. Barry was also named Mortgage Professional of the Year for 2019 by *National Mortgage Professional Magazine*. This is the most prestigious award in the mortgage industry.

Barry has established, grown, and sold many successful businesses. Mortgage Market Guide was a robust rate advisory service and the first of its kind in the industry. In search of modern solutions in the medical industry, Healthcare Imaging Solutions performed high-end medical images such as PET scans for early cancer and heart disease detection. The hugely successful Certified Mortgage Associates was a leading mortgage firm under Barry's guidance. In addition to creating startups, Barry is also a founding partner in Social Survey, the leading reputation management tech company in its space.

During Barry's mortgage sales career, he had the highest annual origination production in the US on two occasions—having originated over $2 billion over the life of his career.

Barry is also the Lead Producer and Managing Partner for the musical *Rock of Ages*—the twenty-seventh longest-running show in Broadway history. While the live show continues to play to sold-out audiences, *Rock of Ages* has also graced the silver screen. In the major motion picture starring Tom Cruise, Barry played the record producer. He has enjoyed working in showbusiness throughout his life and has had speaking roles in several other movies. Recently, he produced Criss Angel's *Mindfreak* at Planet Hollywood in Las Vegas.

About the Author

For over twenty-five years, Barry has been a well-known professional speaker, often addressing the state of the financial and real estate markets to audiences around the world. He regularly ranks as one of the most in-demand speakers on the topics of wealth creation and inspiration—speaking well over eighty times per year.

Barry divides his time between his homes in New Jersey and Florida. He is a father of four.